LIFE IN THE ATHOLL GLENS

Best Wishes

John

28th May 1993

LIFE IN THE ATHOLL GLENS

JOHN KERR

PERTH AND KINROSS DISTRICT LIBRARIES

ISBN 0 905 452 13 5

Published by
Perth and Kinross District Libraries
Shore Road, Perth PH2 8BH

Photography by
John Kerr

Printed by
Cordfall 041 332 4640

CONTENTS

Willie Duff, nicknamed 'Beardy Willie', a gamekeeper and fisherman of repute.

INTRODUCTION

I have been researching Atholl for over twenty five years and during that time acquired an intimate knowledge of the glens. By following ancient tracks I have 'walked into the past' and observed and recorded all the places where the events in this book took place. Information passed on to me by a great many people has been invaluable and I am grateful to them all. Hitherto my research has concentrated on the old roads and tracks in the area and the settlements they served. Now it is the turn of the people who lived in them.

The combined parish of Blair Atholl and Struan is vast and covers nearly six hundred square miles of mountainous terrain, laced by a number of historic glens. Glen Garry, for centuries the main thoroughfare, is the largest and most heavily populated, with Glen Errochty, Glen Bruar, Glen Tilt and Glen Girnaig providing its main feeder rivers. The River Tilt is the most powerful of these and is in turn fed by the River Tarf, the Lochain Burn from Loch Loch and the Fender Burn. These glens form the framework of the book.

There are eighteenth and nineteenth century descriptions of these glens, with many of the places mentioned often supported by modern accounts which act as a backdrop, to provide a setting and dimension to the many tales. Folklore, legend and the supernatural were never very far away in these remote glens, where, up to two hundred years ago, a great many people lived, worked and raised their families. Here are stories of royal hunts, feasts and clan battles, along with tales of the Atholl Highlanders, hillmen and foresters. Blair Castle Charter Room documents, Baron Court records and Kirk Session minutes all combine to give an insight into everyday life in the glens and through eye-witness accounts accurately portray tenants' problems and strifes, poaching incidents, illicit distilling and difficulties encountered at the many corn mills in the area. Early travellers' accounts provide a closer feel of conditions in those days and stories about the churches and local schools are included. The remains of hill forts, standing stones and circles and homesteads, bear witness to past civilisations.

I have translated a great many of the Gaelic place names in the book and those too obscure for me to unravel, I referred to my friend of long standing, Ian Fraser at the School of Scottish Studies, Edinburgh University and I am duly grateful for his continuing assistance. Many of the names indicate the topography and land usage in the district. All the places featured have grid references taken from the Ordnance Survey Pathfinder Series, 1:25000, sheets 66/76; 67/77; 86/96 and 87/97. With this book to hand, readers will be able to explore these glens and perhaps gain an insight into glen life in past centuries.

I must thank all the estate and land owners who have allowed me to tramp freely over their ground in the course of my research and for the help and tolerance shown by keepers, stalkers, shepherds and tenant farmers. My especial thanks go to His Grace The Duke of Atholl, who in addition has allowed me years of research in Blair Castle Charter Room and given permission to reproduce the old photographs and sketches in the book which have come from his archives. I am also grateful to John Cameron of the Atholl Country Collection for the reproduction of some of his photographs. The assistance of my wife Patricia has been invaluable, not only with research in Register House and the National Library of Scotland but in typing the manuscript and proof reading.

Old Struan

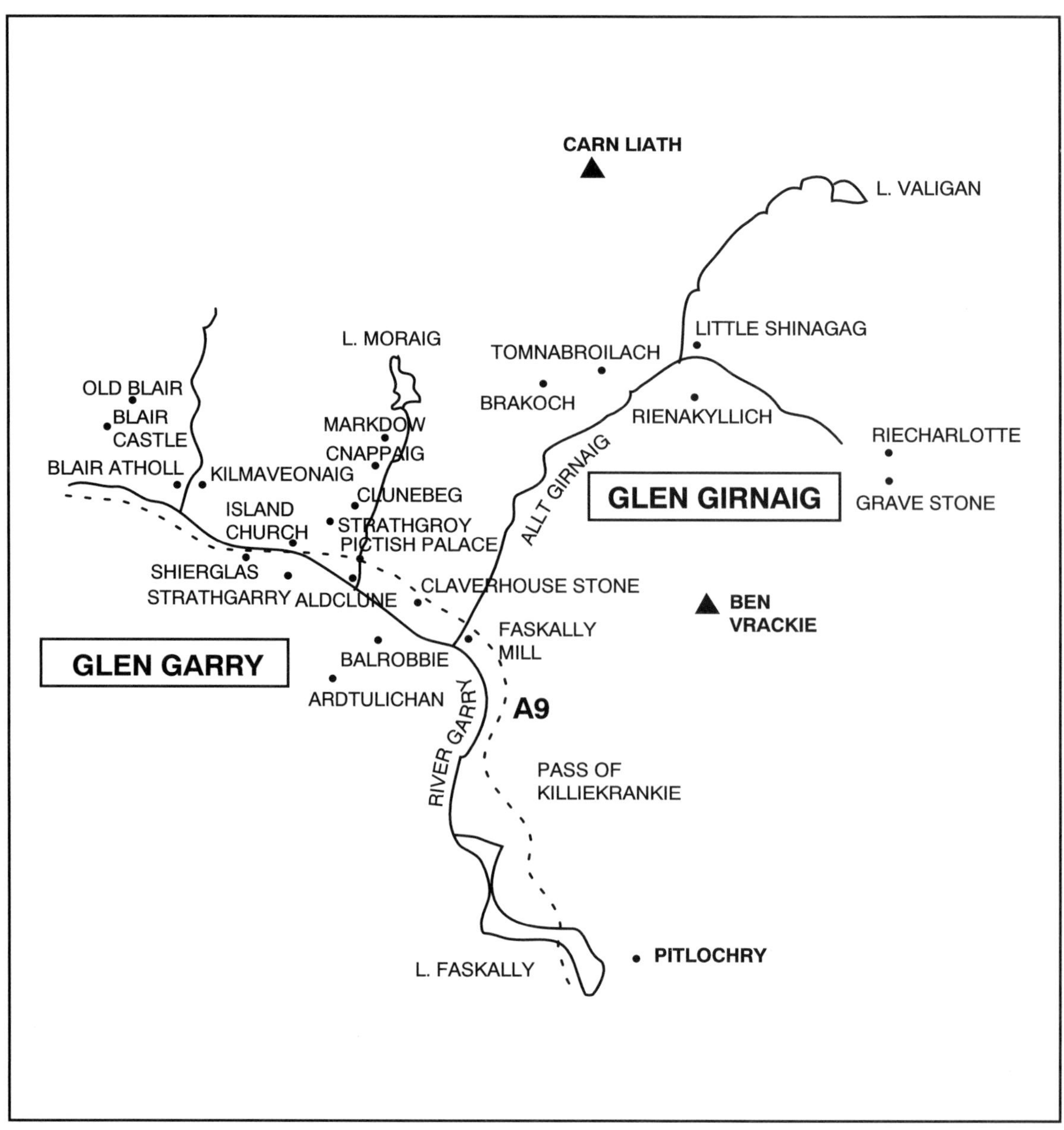
CARN LIATH
L. VALIGAN
LITTLE SHINAGAG
L. MORAIG
TOMNABROILACH
OLD BLAIR
BRAKOCH
BLAIR
CASTLE
MARKDOW
RIENAKYLLICH
CNAPPAIG
RIECHARLOTTE
BLAIR ATHOLL
KILMAVEONAIG
ALLT GIRNAIG
GLEN GIRNAIG
GRAVE STONE
CLUNEBEG
ISLAND
CHURCH
STRATHGROY
PICTISH PALACE
SHIERGLAS
CLAVERHOUSE STONE
STRATHGARRY
ALDCLUNE
BEN
VRACKIE
FASKALLY
MILL
GLEN GARRY
BALROBBIE
ARDTULICHAN
RIVER GARRY
A9
PASS OF
KILLIEKRANKIE
PITLOCHRY
L. FASKALLY

CHAPTER ONE

GLEN GARRY (Part I) & GLEN GIRNAIG

Glen Garry, the most important glen in Atholl, is twenty five miles in length from the Pass of Killiecrankie in the south, to Loch Garry a few miles below the summit at Drumochter to the north. It was described in 1792 as being:

> . . . an extensive strath, constantly tearing its banks and altering its channels. The Garry destroys a fine plain for 6 miles below Strowan. . . In the summer season the face of the country is green, with corn, grass and wood.

Killiecrankie 913 629 lies at the north end of the pass and here, below the old bridge across Allt Girnaig, the Robertsons of Faskally had their corn mill, which was of simple construction with walls of stone and rubble, roofed with straw or heather thatch and turf. It had a vertical water wheel and milled oats and barley for the thirled tenants. Alexander Robertson, the laird of Faskally and several of his tenants were bringing a new millstone down the hill from the quarry at the foot of Ben Vrackie in 1675 when:

Blair Atholl in the 1860s with Blair Castle on the left.

> . . . they were followed and "hotely" pursued by Finlay Fergussone of Baledmond ("ane notorious and commowen murtherer"), John Fergussone of Pitfourie and others, armed with pistols swords guns dirks and other weapons who desired them to desist, otherwise they would cut the "tathers" by which they were drawing the stone; and that the said Finlay Fergussone "drew out ane quhiner and strack att the wholl draught of teathers, and cutted them in betuixt two of the persones drawers thereof comeing downe ane stay brae to the danger of ther lyfes and braikeing of the milne stone. . .

Alexander Robertson made a legal protest at this violent attack but Finlay Fergusson replied that what he had done was 'ane civill interruptione in the Earle of Atholl's name'.

Bringing a millstone down the hill was a serious and sometimes dangerous business at which all the tenants were expected to assist. The brewar (leader) carried the mill wand, a stout oak beam used to axle the stone down the hill. The tenants were on one side of the stone to guide it, while horses tethered to the other, acted as a brake. The brewar was often paid for his services by the tenants hauling loads of peat to his home.

Glen Girnaig

Allt Girnaig joins the River Garry at Killiecrankie while the glen itself runs several miles to the north, with its main catchment area being the southern slopes of the Beinn a' Ghlo mountains.

Tomnabroilach (knoll of the blaeberry) 937 669 is four miles up the glen. The farm house is substantially intact and was inhabited until well into this century. Blaeberries were used for dyeing a violet or purple colour and having an astringent quality were sometimes administered in cases of dysentry. Occasionally the berries were drunk with milk which provided a cool, refreshing drink and at other times they were made into pies and jellies, now and then laced with whisky.

The Mill of Faskally beside the old bridge across Allt Girnaig in 1810. (Sketch by Lady Emily Murray)

In 1719 Margaret Stewart accused Charles McLaren of assaulting her on two occasions at Tomnabroilach: Firstly and while still in his employ, she claimed he pushed her out of a tub of washing and into a nearby stream, while, after she had left, did 'shove' her off a seat. The Lude Baron Court fined McLaren £10 Scots for this 'horseplay'.

An immense sheep roundel built in the 1940s from 500 tons of stone and capable of holding 600 sheep in times of storm, stands beside the house. Much of the stone came from **Brakoch** (speckled place) 933 669 and because of this, little is now visible in this settlement save for the footings of many buildings. It was a large settlement described by Dan MacMillan, who died in the 1960s at the age of 80 years, as having 'eleven smokes'.

A typical Highland croft in Glen Girnaig. (1810 sketch by Lady Emily Murray)

In 1732 a case of assault was heard in the Lude Baron Court between Elspeth, wife of Robert Stewart and Beatrix, wife of John Robertson, both tenants in Brakoch:

> Robert Stewart acknowledges that his wife and John Robertson's wife were scolding one another and that his wife upon that threatened to beat John Robertson's wife and that she defying her they fell into handy blows upon seeing whereof, Robert Stewart got hold of his wife as did John Robertson but before they did so, Robert Stewart's wife was bled at mouth and nose . . .

Elspeth alleged she threatened to beat Beatrix who 'railed at her both to her face and behind her back'. They then started fighting and since 'the other woman got her by the mouth and the nose till she bled she happened to get one or more of her fingers into her mouth and bit it till it bled'. Beatrix denied that she had been scolding Elspeth, merely reproving her for her husband not keeping his lambs out of their corn, when Elspeth 'came full upon her and took all her head cloaths off her giving her bitter and virulent language all the time'. She confessed that in her own defence she indeed 'got hold of Elspeth by the nose until it bled and that three of her fingers were bitten'.

Donald Robertson, John Robertson's son:

> . . . upon seeing his mother in hazard of being hurt he came in a hurry to relieve her and that he got hold of Robert Stewart's wife by the breast endeavouring to carry her off and telling her that the strokes she designed his mother he would rather take himself. Upon which she got hold of him by the hair on each side of his head and pulled him until he bled at the nose and fell down and she above him.

In judgment the Court fined Elspeth and Robert Stewart 'for his interest in bloodwick' £50 Scots payable to Lude for 'stricking and blooding Donald Robertson'. Similarly Beatrix and John Robertson were also to pay £50 to Lude 'of an unlaw [fine] for a bloodwick for stricking and blooding Alspit Stewart,' while both parties were to procure caution 'for their mutual good behaviour'.

Riecharlotte (Charlotte's shieling) 979 655 was probably named after Charlotte, the Lady Lude who entertained 'Bonnie Prince Charlie' at Lude House in 1745. The presence of a gravestone nearby relates to an incident when a coffin party was approaching the shieling from Glen

Gravestone near Riecharlotte, the final resting place for the body being carried to Blair Atholl by a coffin party.

Brerachan, heading for Blair Atholl. A violent snowstorm arose, causing the bearers to scatter for safety and it was six weeks later before they were able to return to safeguard the dead. Rather than disturb him further, they decided he should remain where he had rested for so many weeks. The grave is situated about a hundred yards from the estate track and its stone is a conspicuous landmark in the area.

Glen Garry

A short distance to the north of Killiecrankie and below Urrard House is the **Claverhouse Stone** 908 632, a prominent feature in the field beside the road. Popularly regarded as the site where 'Bonnie' Dundee fell after the Battle of Killiecrankie in 1689, it is more likely to be a standing stone of greater antiquity and past significance. An annual service for the fallen of 1689 is held at a commemorative cairn further up the hill, nearer to the main battle site.

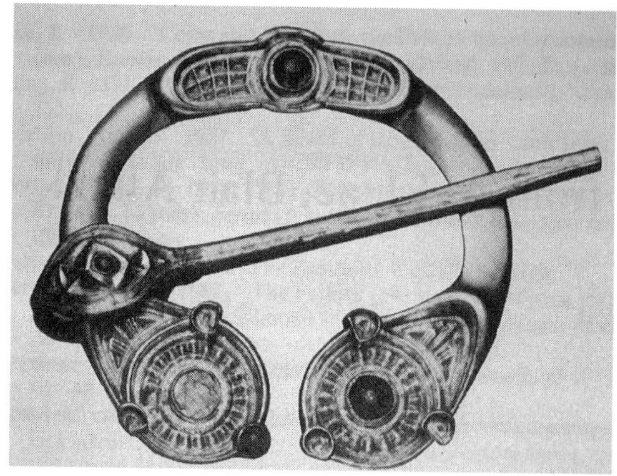

The silver brooch found in the Pictish Palace near Aldclune.

A **Pictish king's palace** 900 640 was located a few hundred yards to the north west of the hamlet of Aldclune until it was completely obliterated by the building of the new A9 in the 1980s. A brief archaeological dig was undertaken prior to the start of construction work and the most significant find was an early ninth century silver brooch,

A service to commemorate the tercentenary of the Battle of Killiecrankie was held at the battle site on 27 July 1989. It was conducted by, left to right: Professor Robin Barbour, interim moderator at Tenandry church; The Rev. James Duncan, minister of Blair Atholl and Struan and Michael Hare Duke, Episcopal Bishop of St Andrews, Dunkeld and Dunblane.

now known as the Aldclune Brooch. It was a significant find of its type and is now housed in the National Museum in Edinburgh.

A burial ground or barrow, the **Sithean** (fairies) 899 649 is a conspicuous landmark on the skyline above Aldclune. It is three hundred feet in circumference, thirty feet high and at one time is said to have been surrounded by a circle of upright stones which were later removed for building purposes.

The Sithean, a conspicuous knoll to which Charles of the Clunes retired to consult the fairies. The Pass of Killiecrankie is in the background.

The following story about the Sithean appears in the manuscript of General Robertson of Lude, c1790:

> Charlach na Chluan, or Charles of the Clunes, was son of John Donaldson, 4th Baron of Lude – He lived at Clunemore where his bed, as it is called, is still shown between two large stones placed in an artificial mound on the high ground above the houses of Clunemore. There, by tradition he is recorded to have consulted the fairies, on all transactions respecting the Country, so that when applied to for advice in cases where injuries had been sustained, by Theft or Robbery, he retired to this mound, where pretending to consult the fairies, he never failed of giving the injured party such advice as occasioned the recovery of their property. By this laudable artifice, so necessary in superstitious times, he obtained reverence from the people, deterring them from crimes, and redress to the injured, which they could not otherwise have obtained. His memory is still held in such esteem that it is deemed unlucky for those who injure his Posterity.

Clunebeg Tenants

Clunebeg (little meadow) 898 644 had six tenants living and working their plots in 1823 and the Atholl Estate factor's comments are more well-disposed than usual:

> **Peter McGlashan** – Not the best subject in the country. Is well employed as a carpenter – a cart and plough maker.
>
> **John Menzies** and **Fergus Menzies** – Tenants in another part.
>
> **Duncan Moon** – a decent tenant. Mason and well employed.
>
> **Finlay Scott** –A decent tenant. Carpenter and well employed.
>
> **Fergus Menzies** – A weaver and well employed.
>
> **Captain Peter Robertson** – A good tenant. Farm well managed.

A cottage near Aldclune c1900. The footings of this thatched cottage are clearly visible beside the stream.

Details of each of these tenants' farm holdings, rent and crop returns for the same year were:

Tenant	Arable acres	Pasture acres	Lease years	Rent £ s d	Crop returns £ s d
Peter McGlashan	5½	4	1	15 0 0	22 11 6
John Menzies etc	1½	1$^{1}/_{10}$	1	20 0 0	6 18 0
Duncan Moon	2½	½	1	6 0 0	9 9 0
Finlay Scott	¾	–	1	3 0 0	3 12 3
Fergus Menzies	¾	–	1	3 0 0	6 15 6
Captain Robertson	42½	22 ½	15	127 6 0	169 15 0
	53½	28 $^{1}/_{10}$	20	£174 6 0	£219 1 3

Three quarters of this settlement of over 81 acres were leased for fifteen years to Captain Robertson and even though he was described as a 'good tenant', his returns were barely viable despite having more security of tenure and considerably more land than the other tenants. It is interesting to note that almost all the tenants had other means of employment at a trade which in some ways reflects the direction of much of Scottish agriculture in the less-favoured areas 170 years later.

At nearby **Strathgroy** 894 648 there was an excellent example of a water-powered threshing mill, the farm being large enough to warrant its installation. The mill dam was built in 1857 by the tenant, Robert Murray who was paid £40 for the preparation work. The sluice gate and underground lade taking the water to the wheel are much in evidence and as late as 1975 the barn machinery was complete with wheels, cogs, belts while the threshing machine itself, supplied by Daniel Douglas of Perth was in use until the mid 1960s and the advent of the combine harvester.

John Stewart was the tenant in 1823 and was described as:

> ...rather an ill-disposed man but a good farmer. Entered into the farm when it was in very bad order and allowed it to get worse by not buying any of his predecessor's crop which was sold off under direction of the Rev. W. Stewart.

Within two years John Stewart had been evicted and became the landlord of the Trinafour Inn. (see page 120).

Remains of the sluice gate for the mill dam at Strathgroy.

Gaunt remains of gable ends in Markdow, home of James Fraser, the illicit distiller. Carn Liath is in the background.

There are a number of settlements on the plateau above Aldclune, one of them being **Cnappaig** (place of lumps) 900 652 and the tenant, Alex Mackenzie, was hopelessly in debt in 1822. He owed the estate £130 and told the factor that he 'has no money nor effects to dispose off at present, nor any victuals to reduce his debt'. His farm was largely arable and that year he had planted oats, barley, pease, turnips, potatoes and lint. In his assessment of tenants the factor, in his more usual vein, described Mackenzie as 'a particularly worthless fellow, and litigious'.

Illicit Distilling

Markdow (black merk land) 903 657 is the highest settlement in the glen at over 1,000 feet and its remains are immense with several gable ends still complete. James Fraser, the tenant in 1802, was caught distilling whisky illicitly and his copper still and two bolls of malt were removed. He was summoned to appear in the Weem Excise Court. In his defence he explained that he had thought it imperative to distil a little whisky for the comfort of a sick person on the farm but concluded: 'It turned out to be my great loss'.

Balrobbie Farm (Robertstown) 906 628, now part of the RSPB bird reserve, lies south of the River Garry from Killiecrankie. A character called Peter Robertson was born here in 1809 and his early life was spent in farming and illicit distilling which was the main revenue for the farm. Ten shillings were paid for every boll (about 140lb.) of malt converted into whisky, with the owner of the malt running the risk of imprisonment, if caught. Peter had a lengthy association with the Atholl Estate and in his youth was apprenticed to Willie Duff, the renowned Dunkeld ghillie and worthy. He served under four dukes and he was part of the guard of honour at Blair Atholl church when Queen Victoria attended the service there in 1844.

His activities in illicit distilling ended in 1859 when a youth spotted the 'pot' hidden under a rock and reported him to the gauger (excise officer). However his method of operation was so discreet that another eighteen months elapsed before the rest of the equipment including the worm and lead were discovered. In the same year he became associated with his cousin, John Robertson, known as 'Drover Robertson' from the nearby farm of Ardtulichan. His duties now lay in travelling as far away as Stornoway and then droving five to six hundred head of Highland cattle as far south as Suffolk, selling them in the many markets on the way.

When a police force was established in Highland Perthshire in the middle of the last century, Peter was appointed as one of the first constables and stationed in Blair Atholl. Later he was transferred to Alyth, where he only stayed a month. When questioned about this, he said: 'Folks made oot I had too many freens aboot and that I wisn'a hard enough on them'. He died at the age of 91 in Wester Balrobbie.

Strathgarry Estate is a mile upstream, also on the south bank of the Garry. It contains the main dwelling, **Strathgarry House** 891 639 and its walled garden was built by Alexander Stewart, the fifth laird, at the turn of the nineteenth century. Close by is the old farm steading which has recently been converted into a concert hall.

A Pictish homestead, called the **Black Castle of Strathgarry** 889 631 lies half way up the hillside above and is now in the midst of a modern plantation. It comprised of a large fortified hut circle measuring 83 feet (26m) by 72 feet (22m) with a 9 feet 6 inches (3m) thick wall which spread out to form a bank over 12 feet across (3.75m). On the open hillside above the plantation the remaining evidence of extensive ancient field systems are clearly visible, while a **stone circle** 889 629, originally of four standing stones, of which three remain, sits a few hundred yards further up the hill.

The Stewart association with Strathgarry began in 1513 when Walter Bannerman granted to John Stewart, 2nd Earl of Atholl, the lands of Strathgarry in exchange for the red cloak he was wearing at the time.

In 1708 the land was feued to the Rev. Duncan Stewart, born around 1650, who from his first marriage produced two sons, Alex and Allan and four daughters. Duncan had been educated at Glasgow university and was appointed the Episcopal minister of Dunoon Parish between 1686 and 1691, when he was deposed for not praying for William and Mary. From 1710 to 1718 he was the minister of Kilmaveonaig Church and not only offered up thanksgiving for the safe arrival of the Pretender but played a major part from the pulpit in influencing his congregation to rise up for him in 1715.

Shierglas Violence

Shierglas (lasting stream) 884 643 is just up-river from Strathgarry and a hundred years ago was in a detached part of the parish of Dull. The principal dwelling house was erected in 1728 and was a fine two-storey laird's house in the shape of a 'T'. Both it and the farm steading to the rear which dates from 1799 are now very much overshadowed by the workings of the adjacent limestone quarry.

For centuries Shierglas was another stronghold of the Stewarts. In 1611 Neil Stewart and others were the subject of a complaint from the Lord Advocate 'for resetting and intercommuning' with James, Earl of Atholl. Resetting at that time was the crime of harbouring a person who had committed an offence and intercommuning was having correspondence with someone denounced in law. It appears that four years earlier, the Earl and his accomplices, armed with 'jacks, steelbonnets, platesleeves, hagbuts and pistolets' broke into the abbey at Coupar Angus and forcibly removed the abbot, Patrick Stirling and his family. None of the defenders appeared in court and all were accused of being rebels.

James Stewart and his servant Donald Cattanach were accused with others in 1760 of committing 'diverse and sundry acts of violence and outrage, to the great oppression and terror of the country in general'. They were part of a recruiting gang, headed by John Stewart of Bonskeid, who during the night of 20 April:

> . . . did in the most illegal manner assault the house of said Donald Seaton when all the family were in bed, and entered the same, all and each of them were guilty of the greatest barbarity exercised upon the person of the said Beatrix Seaton who was thrown on the ground with such violence and trampled upon that three ribs of her right side were broke . . . and did in a most illegal manner sease the said Donald Seaton himself, carry him by force to a considerable distance from his house and keep him in custody till an opportunity offered for making his escape.

The gang also broke into the house of John MacLauchlan during the early morning of the next day and carried off his servant, Donald MacDonald as a hostage, hoping to force MacLauchlan to enlist. The sheriff awarded damages of £2 to Donald Seaton and 10 shillings to John MacLauchlan, with costs of £4.16.0.

The Shierglas estate crossed the River Garry to include Shierglas Island, also known as King's Island, reached by an old ford from below the big house. Just downstream from the confluence with the River Tilt, the Garry at one time curved northwards through what is now the golf course, until it reached the road at the Craggan Corner and then divided to form King's Island. Traditionally this is named after Robert the Bruce who is said to have encamped here with his army on his way to Dalchosnie at the start of the fourteenth century.

Island Church

At the eastern end of the **Island**, 889 645 there is 'a beautiful spot bounded on the south side by the Garry and surrounded with weeping birches and

The Island Church on King's Island during a flood.

other woods of indigenous growth,' and this became the setting for the first Free Church in Blair Atholl. At a meeting on 13 February 1843, a large number of people resolved to form a congregation of the Free Church and as no building was available, they arranged to hold their service in the open air, providing the minister with a preaching tent. Landowners, presumably the heritors of the established church, were strongly against this and demanded that 'the Free Church

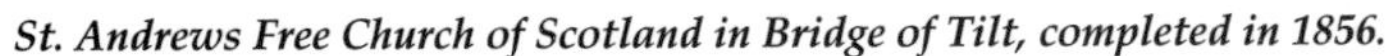

St. Andrews Free Church of Scotland in Bridge of Tilt, completed in 1856.

must be put down', so that the congregation realised that it had to find a permanent site for a church. The tenant of King's Island sympathised with the Free Church and agreed to allow them to erect a temporary meeting place at the eastern end of his ground. He was observed 'industriously and determinedly cutting down and clearing away the underwood which grew upon the place'. The manager of the local saw mill was forbidden to supply him with timber, but on hearing of their plight, the Marquis of Breadalbane offered to provide sufficient wood and also to deliver it from Taymouth. A wooden building, called the Island Church, was started in November 1843 and completed the following spring. The site of the church was below the flood level of the Garry and yet, despite being frequently cut off by the water, there was only one instance when a service could not be held. However, the ravages of the weather and constant flooding seriously damaged the foundations and in 1855 a site was obtained in Bridge of Tilt where St Andrews Church was completed the following year, to house a congregation of between four and five hundred people. The guiding hand through this chapter of the Free Church in Blair Atholl was the Rev. Atholl Stewart, ordained a minister in 1844:

> He upheld its cause amidst many difficulties, preaching in the open air during the years of the disruption and afterwards at King's Island in a wooden erection known as the "Island Church". He laboured earnestly and increasingly for the good of his people until ill-health caused him to resign on 30 March 1882 and he died on 13 September 1894.

St Andrews remained in use until the 1950s. Thereafter the main church and later the tower, were demolished.

The tenants in both Strathgarry and Shierglas were obliged to take their corn to the Mill of Blair for grinding and as the ferry at Boat of Blair was inadequate, plans were drawn up to build a bridge over the river. Subscriptions were raised by two millers, Patrick MacGlashan and Gregor Murray to the sum of over £100. The **bridge** 871 649 was designed to have a central arch of 42 feet and two side arches, each of 35 feet and was completed in 1737 but had fallen down by the next year,

Extract from 'Plan for Blair in Atholl' by Chas. Esplen 1744, showing the Garry Bridge built in 1737, 'two arches of which are fal'n.'

probably in a severe spring spate. Part of the buttresses can still be seen on each bank of the river, beside the footbridge built over a hundred years ago. After 1738 a much improved ferry and a ford, still in occasional farm use, replaced the broken-down bridge. To this day the road leading down towards the river is called Ford Road.

Queen Victoria crossed the Garry by this ford in 1844 as her diary recorded:

> Wednesday, September 18
> At nine o'clock we set off on ponies to go up one of the hills, Albert riding the dun pony and I the gray, attended only by Lord Glenlyon's excellent servant, Sandy McAra, in his Highland dress. We went out by the back way across the road and to the left through the ford, Sandy leading my pony and Albert following closely, the water reaching up above Sandy's knees.

Queen Victoria, dressed in black with a shepherd's tartan shawl and riding a grey Highland pony,

Queen Victoria and Prince Albert fording the Garry with Sandy McAra in 1844.

Sandy McAra as head keeper in 1860.

with Albert, clad in plaid trousers, shooting jacket and white hat, rode out from Blair Castle at nine in the morning, escorted solely by Sandy McAra, an Atholl hillman. He led the royal pair through the Garry Ford, on past a field of turnips to climb to the top of Tulach Hill, which at 1,500 feet, (460m) dominates Blair Atholl from the south. With only a stalwart Highlander as a guide, someone was heard to remark: 'She kens brawly she's in the Hielands. Naebody'll hurt her here.' Lady Charlotte Canning, Lady in Waiting, recorded that Sandy was very proud of being the Queen's guide and no one could persuade him to talk about it. 'It's no for me to tell all that Her Majesty talked about', he said.

Blair Atholl Mills

The Blair Atholl **corn mill** 872 652 is beside Ford Road and has changed little since it was 'modernised' in the 1840s. It appears on Timothy Pont's map of 1600 and in the beginning was a single-storey building made from locally available building material. The roof was of straw thatch and turf placed on a frame of branches and it was cramped and inefficient, needing frequent rebuilding. It was known as 'Katherine's Mill', after Lady Katherine Hamilton who became the first Duchess of Atholl in 1703.

An 1810 sketch of the Blair Atholl corn mill before it was enlarged in the 1840s. A lint mill is on the right. (Sketch by Lady Emily Murray)

Atholl Highlanders escorting Queen Victoria and Prince Albert to church in Blair Atholl in 1844.

Two escaped prisoners, Alex MacDonald from Tulloch and James Robertson from Urrard Beg, broke into the mill and stole four bolls of meal and some barley. At their trial they pleaded guilty and were ordered to pay the price of the stolen meal, expenses of the prosecution and in addition, were fined two guineas. Further, they were banished from the area and told that if they ever returned, they would be sentenced to three months in prison and whipped every Friday through the streets of Logierait, where the courthouse and jail were then located.

Just before the time of Queen Victoria's visit, the old mill was finally pulled down and a new one built, which is more or less the one we know today. At the time it was described as being:

> . . . one of the most substantial benefits by the erection of a mill and kiln at Blair upon the most improved principles of construction.

Blair Atholl parish church was built in 1825, beside the newly re-routed main road to the north. Queen Victoria and Prince Albert attended divine service on Sunday 15 September 1844, the minister, Mr Irvine, being informed that it should not last for more than one and a half hours, and that the Queen was used to a sermon of no longer than twenty five minutes. The royal pew, slightly raised and opposite the pulpit, was handsomely lined with crimson satin, cushioned and carpeted. The Queen, who insisted that Lady Glenlyon sat next to her in the pew to help her follow the service to which she was not accustomed, wore a black satinette gown and mantle and a white bonnet. She listened intently to the sermon, taken from St. Matthew, chapter 5, verse 13: 'Ye are the salt of the earth.'. It was a 'plain, straightforward discourse, devoid of all flourishes of rhetoric'.

Kilmaveonaig (church of St Beoghna) 879 657 is a small Episcopalian church now standing alone, surrounded by fields, below Lude House. Up to the 1820s this was a flourishing village consisting of ten houses and barns clustered round the church, school and an inn where the Red Comyn is reputed to have developed a taste for Atholl ale in the thirteenth century (see page 103). In the early nineteenth century the school had up to 120 scholars who were taught by a man called

Seaton who had been injured in a rock fall at Toldunie. Gradually Kilmaveonaig village fell into decay as new cottages were built beside the new main road at Ballentoul, leaving only the church to survive.

Lady Charlotte Canning, Lady in Waiting and Lady Caroline Cox, Maid of Honour to Queen Victoria, attended service in the church in 1844:

> Car and I went in the evening to the poor little Episcopal Chapel. It has bare earth between the seats and only a board to stand or kneel upon and a pathway paved. The galleries crowd it up and it might hold a number of people but only 12 were there including the clergy man.

Theft and Affray

In the Lude Baron Court on 24 August 1700, Donald and Alex Robertson accused John Clerk from Dunkeld of needless assault when they went to the rescue of Jonat McGlashan at the Kilmaveonaig Market:

> . . . the said Johne Clerk did take ane gripe of Jonat McGlashine in Kindrochit ryping her alledging that she was stealing in waers to the Mercat [Kilmaveonaig] to sell custom free and did take his coat from hir aledging she was to sell it. And I the said Donald Robertson went to help her. The sd. Johne Clerk did throw me down and brused my mouth and nose and bled me. And I the sd. Alex Robertson seeing my brother so abused I did take up ane stone and did strike the sd. Johne Clerk on the head and Bled him and wounded him, and the said Johne did strik the sd. Alex with ane Staff on the Arm that is terribly swelled that I am not able to win my living. . .

John Gow, a witness to the affray, claimed he 'did see Johne Clerk take the cott from Jonat McGlashan and ane kebik [cheese]. . .' John Clerk was fined £20 Scots and the two brothers were ordered to pay £40 Scots and to pay for 'curing of Clerk's wound'. Donald Robertson was fined an extra £10 'for being the instrument of the play and ryott. . .'

'The four carpenter lads' in 1858. Left to right:Sandy McDougall, James Douglas, head carpenter, James Bell, David Lowe.

Blair Castle

Blair Castle 856 661 is at the heart of the land of Atholl and its history spans over 700 years. Tradition states that when the Earl of Atholl was away fighting in the Crusades, John, the Red Comyn invaded Atholl in 1269 and built Comyn's Tower, which is now incorporated in the north-west part of the main castle building. It was enlarged in the sixteenth century and although a fortress, its use then was mainly as a hunting lodge. John Stewart, 3rd Earl of Atholl and famous for his hospitality, built on a two-storey extension which included a large banqueting hall. Immediately after the '45, the 2nd Duke set about rebuilding and restoring the castle, but he was determined that never again would it be a fortress and garrisoned. Plans were drawn up to 'clip' the castle, which was reduced in height by two storeys, while battlements, pepper-box turrets and crow-step gables were removed, so that after ten years it resembled a large, square-plan Georgian mansion.

In 1803 William Wordsworth the poet, and his sister Dorothy, made a tour of Scotland. Of their visit to Blair she recorded:

Blair castle as a fortress before 1747.

We rested upon the heather seat which Burns was so loth to quit that moonlight evening when he first went to Blair Castle, and had a

Atholl House, like a large Georgian house, in 1810. (Sketch by Lady Emily Murray)

Pipers and drummers of the Atholl Highlanders on parade outside Blair Castle in 1895.

> pleasure in thinking that he had been under the same shelter and viewed the little waterfall opposite. . . The castle has been modernized, which has spoilt its appearance. It is a large irregular pile, and even noble before it was docked of its battlements and whitewashed.

In 1869 major alterations and rebuilding were carried out under the directions of the 7th Duke, following the plans of Bryce, the Edinburgh architect. He added the battlements and turrets in the Scottish baronial style to make it the castle we know today.

Atholl Highlanders

The Atholl Highlanders were formed as a regiment in 1777 when the 4th Duke offered to raise a thousand men to serve for three years in America during the War of Independence. The regiment never embarked for America but was instead posted to Ireland as the 77th Foot of the Line, returning in 1782. Next year they were ordered to India and marched to Portsmouth for embarkation, but fearing a mutiny as the three-year enlistment had long since ended, the regiment was sent on to Berwick and disbanded. The next time the Atholl Highlanders were called up was for ceremonial duty in 1822 when George IV paid his state visit to Edinburgh, and 98 officers and men lined the route as part of the official welcome.

At the time of Queen Victoria's visit, their standard bearer was Willie Duff, a 6 foot 3 inches tall Highlander sporting a luxuriant beard, which earned him the nickname of 'Beardy Willie'. He was described as 'a savage, picturesque keeper with a long black beard' who entered the service of the Atholl family in 1839. He was a gamekeeper, fisherman of repute and a noted bard who made violins and 'cellos in his spare time. During the

Tents and marquees at the Atholl Gathering, 7 September 1857.

Queen's three-week stay in Blair Castle in 1844, the Atholl Highlanders acted as her guard for which they were rewarded the following year by the presentation of colours and the right to bear arms. Today the Atholl Highlanders are the only remaining private army in Europe with this privilege.

One of the social highlights of the year was the Atholl Gathering, which until 1846 was called the Tilt Gathering and was held in Bridge of Tilt. In that year however, it was held in the grounds of Blair Castle for the first time and continued there until 1913 and the outbreak of the Great War. The Gathering was revived in 1984 and now takes place annually in the Target Park beside the main castle drive on the last Sunday in May.

Daniel Defoe visited Old Blair in 1769 and described what he saw:

> The town consists of only a few peat houses, except the minister's house, a pretty good change or public House and a poor old kirk, the pews all broken down, doors open, full of dirt. The minister preaches once a week.

The ruins of St. Bride's church in Old Blair in 1860, with part of the roof still intact.

St. Bride's Church 867 665 was featured in the Bagimond Rolls of the thirteenth century, when it was shown as paying a tithe of four merks (£2.13s.4d) to Rome in 1275 and is therefore an ancient parish of some importance. As well as being the former main church of the Atholl family, it contains the vault in which Viscount 'Bonnie'

Minigaig Street (c.1900) in Old Blair, at the start of the Minigaig Pass route across the Grampians.

Blair Atholl in the 1840s.

Dundee was buried after the Battle of Killiecrankie. The two hundredth anniversary of this battle was commemorated in 1889 when the 7th Duke unveiled an inscribed memorial tablet to Viscount Dundee on the inner face of the south wall. A special anniversary service to mark the three hundredth year since the battle was held in 1989 when Professor Robin Barbour and other leading churchmen conducted an open-air service beside the ruined church, having walked there from the battle site.

Rain in Atholl

The broken Kirk is dank and green,
the Hill wind sobs, the fir tree weeps,
And a whittret, slim and lank and lean,
Slinks by where Clavers sleeps.

From the grim mist where Urrard lies
The birches burst like armed men,
And the wild cateran-tempest cries
The slogan down the glen.

The clouds, like gathering eagles, wing
Above Garry pools, awhirl
With brown blood shed when James was King.

. . .

Here smiles a snowdrop girl.

J B Salmond

Around the year 1475, Angus of Islay raided Atholl and Sir John Stewart, the 1st Earl and his wife, Countess Eleanor Sinclair took refuge in the church, but were dragged from the altar and taken captive back to Islay. A great storm arose during the sea crossing, wrecking many of the galleys, with the subsequent loss of much of the plunder. Believing this to be a sign of divine judgment on him for the sacrilege he had committed in St. Bride's, Angus liberated his prisoners, and barefoot and stripped to the waist, undertook a return pilgrimage with the remaining salvaged spoils to the church, where he performed a humiliating penance.

The elders of the Kirk Session laid down very strict regulations about conduct on the Sabbath:

> Blair Athol May 1st 1720
> . . . No traveller should travel with baggage on the Sabbath day, that their baggage should be taken away from them till Sabbath was over. And that those without a reasonable excuse absent, or stay from Divine Service on the Lord's Day should be fined. The Session appoints to send to the Clerk of Court to get an extract of the Act, and it should be read publickly in the church here for preventing the likewise in the future. . .

Blair Town, now **Old Blair** 867 656 provided eleven men for the Duke of Atholl's Fencibles, a form of local militia, in 1705 and 1706 and by 1760 the community included: Lauchlan McLauchlan, shoemaker; Donald Robertson, schoolmaster; Robert Robertson, merchant; Robert Anderson, smith and Donald Donaldson, wright. The last named took up residence in 1759 and served 'most gentlemen between Logyrate and Dalnacardoch' as a wright. He married a Miss Spinks who had remained in the family house after her father had departed, until his housekeeper, Mrs Bradshaw, 'was suitably provided'. When it was time for Miss Spinks to leave, Donald arrived with a horse and cart, and failing to alert Mrs Bradshaw to open the front door, removed his bride's belongings and chest through a downstairs window. Just then Mrs Bradshaw 'appeared in a passion', believing that thieves were at work, and although the contents of the chest were shown to her, she remained unconvinced.

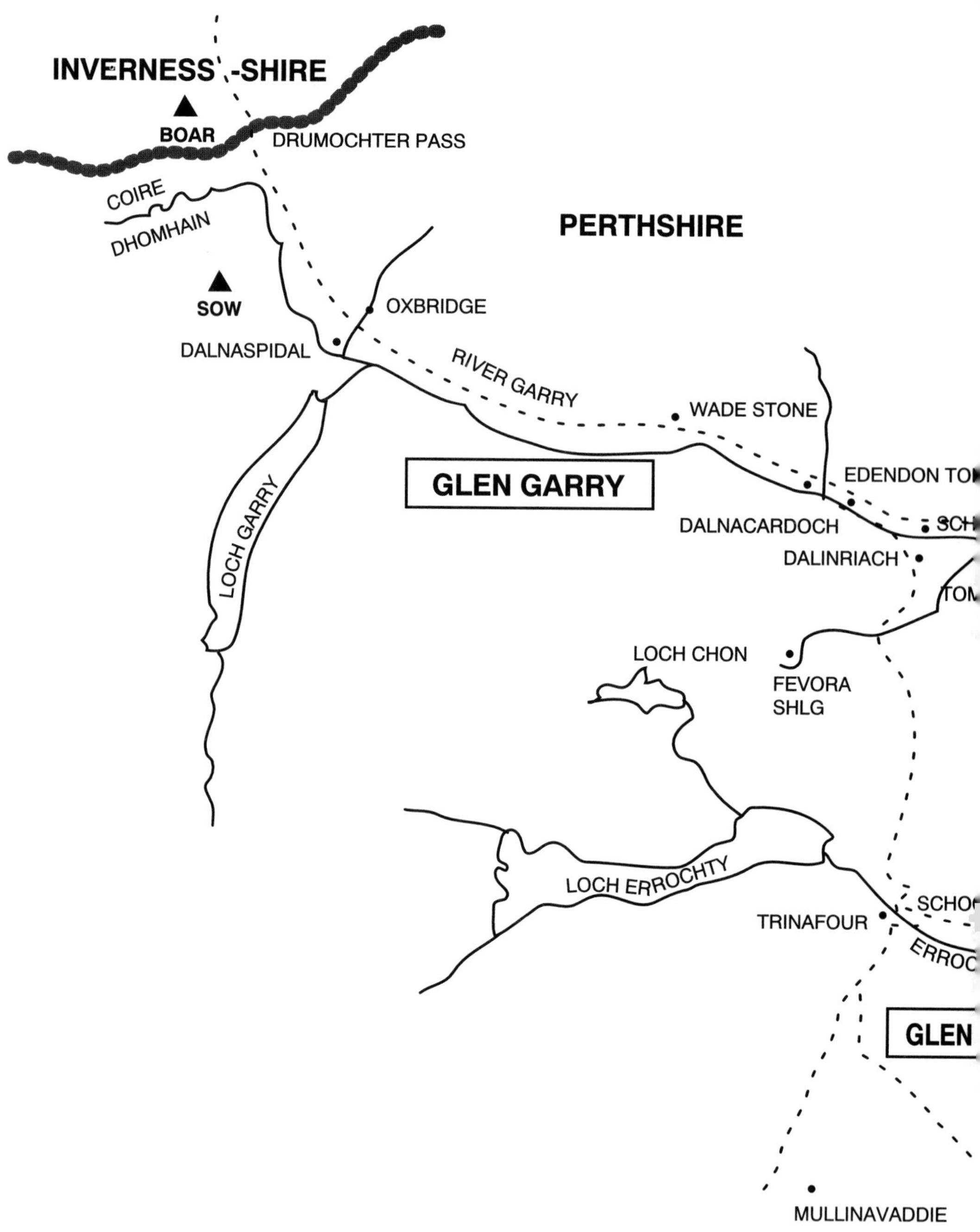
INVERNESS-SHIRE
BOAR
DRUMOCHTER PASS
COIRE DHOMHAIN
PERTHSHIRE
SOW
OXBRIDGE
DALNASPIDAL
RIVER GARRY
WADE STONE
GLEN GARRY
LOCH GARRY
EDENDON
DALNACARDOCH
DALINRIACH
LOCH CHON
FEVORA SHLG
LOCH ERROCHTY
TRINAFOUR
GLEN
MULLINAVADDIE

CHAPTER TWO

GLEN GARRY (Part II)

In 1731 the 2nd Duke began to landscape the grounds around the castle by building parks and pleasure grounds, paths and roads. Hercules Park was laid out in the 1740s with fruit trees, ornamental ponds and statues.

After a long and tedious walk, Dorothy Wordsworth described it thus in 1803:

. . .We went into the garden, where there was plenty of fruit - gooseberries, hanging as thick as possible upon the trees, ready to drop off; I thought the gardener might have invited us to refresh ourselves with some of his fruit after our long fatigue. One part of the garden was decorated with statues, "images," as poor Mr Gill used to call those at Racedown, dressed in gay-painted clothes; and in a retired corner of the grounds, under some tall trees, appeared the figure of a favourite old gamekeeper of one of the former Dukes, in the attitude of pointing his gun at the game – "reported to be a striking likeness," said the gardener.

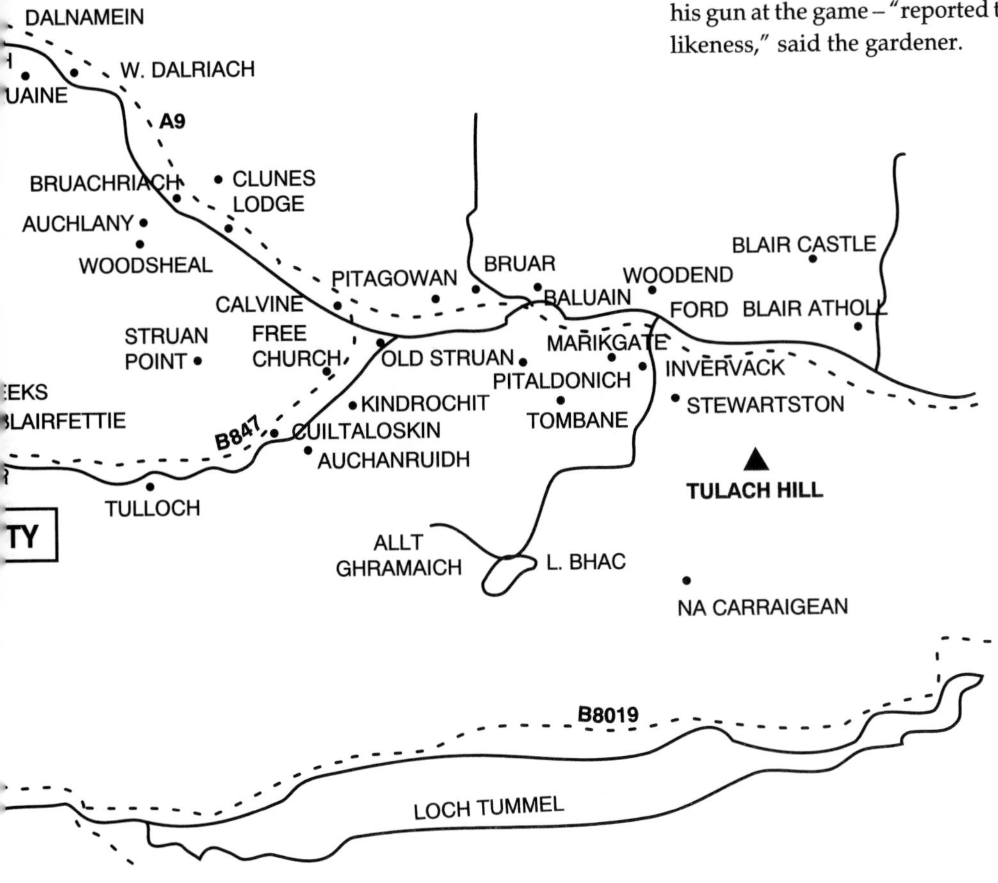

A fine pair of wrought iron gates in the south wall of Hercules Park, being admired by the 8th Duke of Atholl (Bardie) and his wife Kitty, on the occasion of their silver wedding on 20 July 1924.

The second rink in the curling club league. Left to right: Thomas Jack holding the Duchess Anne Broom; William Fleming, auctioneer; Robert Grant, hotel keeper; Robert Jack, slater.

Curling is first mentioned as taking place in an organised way in Atholl in 1692 and by the nineteenth century was a well-established winter sport. On many a winter's day the tranquillity of Hercules Park was shattered by the shouts and cries of curlers as the rink in the park was part of the Dunkeld Curling Club league, formed in 1834. Duchess Anne, wife of the 6th Duke, was one of the sport's great enthusiasts and she presented the 'Duchess Anne' Broom in 1853, a trophy which was hotly contested for by all the competing rinks in the area.

Last Public Hanging

The Balvenie Pillar is situated on the top of **Tom na Croiche** (the hangman's knoll) and marks the spot where the last public hanging in Atholl took

Curling in Hercules Park in the last century.

The Balvenie Pillar built in 1755 on top of the Hangman's Knoll to commemorate the last public hanging in Blair Atholl in 1630.

place in 1630. It was erected by James, the 2nd Duke in 1755 on the spot where the executions were carried out.

John Stewart from Auchgobhal in Glen Tilt murdered a man called Shorry because of the contempt and disrespect shown by him. A number of men were sent out from Blair Castle to arrest him but on reaching Auchgobhal found him barricaded in his house and armed with a loaded gun which he threatened to use if approached. It was therefore decided to starve him out and on the second day he said he would give himself up to a man from Dalvorist (further up Glen Tilt). Eventually he was taken captive down to the castle and as they were shutting the dungeon door on him, he said to them:

You may enclose me in this cell,
Until I stink within its wall,
Howe'er my conduct I bewail,
Poor Shorry I can ne'er recall.

During his imprisonment many rejoiced, none more so than a man called McIntosh, a forester in Glen Tarf, whose beat adjoined Stewart's. Perhaps through the good offices of the Earl of Atholl, Stewart was freed and on hearing of McIntosh's delight at his expense, plotted his revenge. He invited McIntosh and his ghillie to spend a day's shooting on one of the Beinn a'Ghlo mountains and afterwards they spent the night in a bothy at **Coire Rainich** (ferny corrie) 958 755. In the middle of the night Stewart took his revenge on McIntosh by stabbing him through the heart and then asked his own servant to kill the ghillie. This he was most reluctant to do, but fearing for his own life, stabbed him several times, taking care that none would be fatal. The ghillie, realising what was going on, struggled a little and then feigned death. They then threw the supposed lifeless body on top of McIntosh and made off. They had not gone far when Stewart observed that to make it look more as if they had killed each other, the ghillie's body should be underneath rather than on top , so they returned to the bothy and were in the process of rearranging the bodies when Stewart became suspicious that perhaps the ghillie was not dead after all. He slashed at the soles of his feet several times with his dirk, but somehow the ghillie, by an almost superhuman act of self control, kept motionless and Stewart departed, convinced that his evil deed had been satisfactorily concluded. When he felt it was safe to do so, the ghillie managed to crawl down to **Dail Fheannach** (shaggy haugh) and raise the alarm over the murder of his master.

When the news that the ghillie had survived reached Stewart, he fled to Caithness where he started up a school. The Earl of Atholl was determined to capture him and bring him to justice, so he sent a man called Ferguson, dressed as a beggar, to seek him out. When Stewart's whereabouts were discovered, the Earl selected thirty three of his most trustworthy men and sent them north with Ferguson as their guide. On their arrival at the place, they learned that Stewart was at a party in a nearby inn, so Ferguson entered and drank his health. This was a sign to the Atholl men and they rushed in and grabbed him. As he was being secured, he made up a plaintive Gaelic song which runs as follows:

Curs't be the beer that banished my fear,
Till they caught inawares at the Ball me,
The 30 and 3 chased my swiftness from me,
Then to prison with ropes they did have me.

Despite many schemes to escape on the journey from Caithness to Blair Atholl, these were to no avail. On one occasion, on the Minigaig Pass, he asked if he could be allowed to shoot a deer, but his request was refused. He languished in the dungeon at the castle for several months, before he was hanged on the gibbet on Tom na Croiche, where:

> His body was allowed to hang there while the sinews kept the skeleton together. It is said when the wind was high the rattling of these would be heard at a great distance. When his wife passed or repassed the place she used to cover her face with her plaid as she could not bear such an awful spectacle.

The penultimate hanging on Tom na Croiche concerned a ploughman, who, as a result of an argument, killed the farmer at **Fas-Charaidh** (rough stance) 891 704 and buried the body in a bog between there and **Druim nam Beathaichean** (ridge of the beasts) 895 705, on the grassy, upland plateau above Glen Tilt. A few days later, on a Sunday, the body was uncovered by a neighbouring farmer's dog and this startling news was related to the congregation on their way to church. When the ploughman overheard this, he made a pretence of having forgotten his bible and turned back as if to fetch it, but he instead fled towards Invervack where he was captured and in due course brought to justice by being hanged on Tom na Croiche.

The Whim 869 670, built in 1762, stands on a commanding ridge overlooking the castle from the north, and when the 2nd Duke told the parish minister that he was at a loss as to what he should call it, the Rev. Mr Stewart replied that it would be difficult as it was but a 'whim'. In the fashion of the time, it is a sham fort from which at one time was flown the three-legged banner of the Isle of Man, indicating the family's association with that island.

Castle Grounds

Plans for landscaping the ground round the castle were well in hand by the 1740s. The settlements on **Tulach** (hill) 865 650 were the first to be included in the policies as the landscape designer was anxious to extend the grounds across the River Garry to give dimension and scale to the overall design of the pleasure grounds. Two avenues of trees were planted to line up with the castle and traces of them can still be seen despite the ravages of time and the new A9. A semi-circular perimeter dyke was built round the upper edge and emphasised with trees. Much of this boundary and its trees, mainly beech, still remains.

In April 1747 it was reported that four stots (bullocks between two and four years old) had been stolen from the 'Parks of Tulloch', by thieves from Rannoch. A gang of them was operating in the area, mostly Camerons, led by a John Cameron, known as 'Cameron Mor'. They were all deserters either from Lord George Murray's or the Earl of Loudon's regiments, who had failed to hand over their arms after Culloden.

Stewartston or **Balnasteuartach** 843 650 lies to the west of Tulach. In 1602 Patrick Stewart, his brother John and their servant Alastair Reoch lived there and were brought to trial for the killing of another servant, Angus Dubh McIvor,

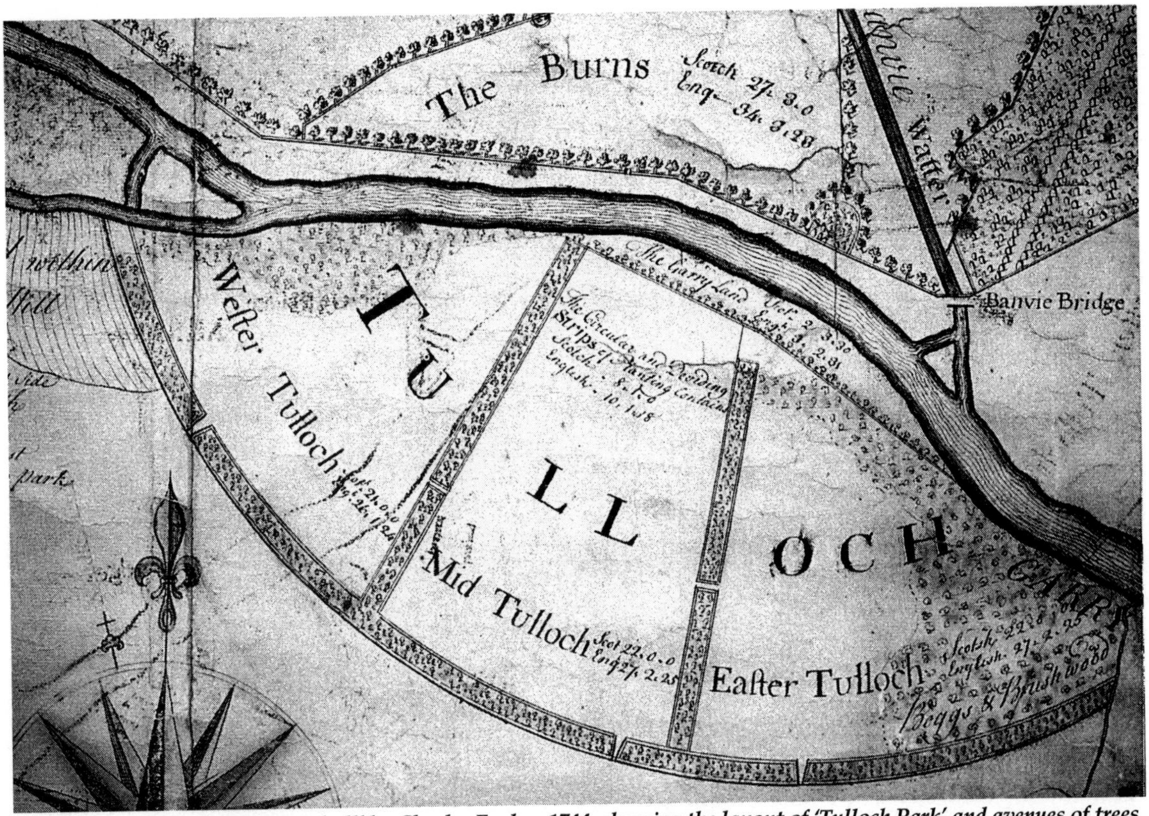

Extract from 'Plan of Blair in Atholl' by Charles Esplen, 1744, showing the layout of 'Tulloch Park' and avenues of trees. Four stots were stolen from here in 1747.

whom they accused of assaulting Patrick's daughter. The three men bound Angus so that he could not escape, then broke his right leg with an axe, going on to mutilate him viciously with a dirk. They then put him on a horse and took him to Blair Atholl where he died five days later.

At the trial Patrick was found guilty of murder and sentenced to be 'ta'en to ane place byside the Mercat Cross of Edinburgh and thair his heid to be stryken fra his bodie and all his movabill guidis to be escheit'.

Apparently in those times the courts did not take mitigating circumstances into consideration.

By 1820 there was only one tenant at **Woodend** 845 659, John Stewart, who paid £50 for Woodend, Black Isle and Boat of Invervack. Nothing remains of the ferry today except one reminder in the name of a field on the south bank of the Garry, the Bell Park, where once the bell for summoning the ferryman was located.

Ath Bhaird Suainidh (ford of the Sunart bard) 843 658 was situated a few hundred yards downstream from the ferry. Sometime in the sixteenth century a marauding party of men from Sunart in Argyll were retreating across the river with their loot at this place from their raid in Atholl, when the bard was shot dead by an arrow and the ford was named after him. The remainder of the party was later captured on the hill above Bohespic where the spot was marked by cairns which are now lost in modern plantations.

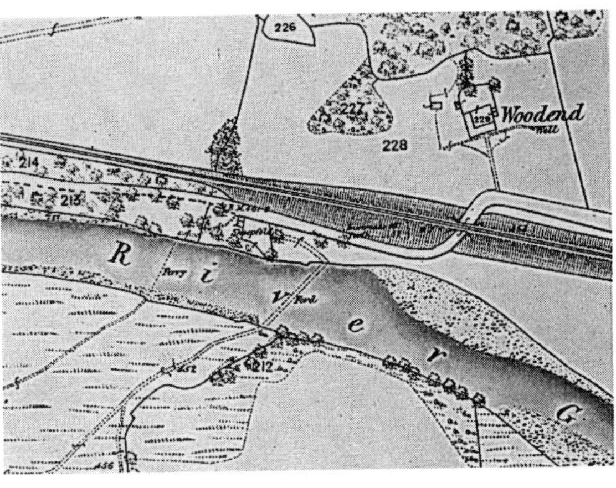

Extract from the First Edition Ordnance Survey map showing the Ath Bhaird Suainidh ford and nearby Woodend ferry.

Invervack Farm in the last century.

Invervack Settlements

One of the old routes from Atholl to Tummelside started from the ford and ferry, passed through the lands of Invervack, over by Loch Bhac before descending to Grenich on Tummel. The land of Invervack was a detached part of the Barony of Struan (see page 111) and 250 years ago contained six settlements. Now it is difficult to imagine it at that time, with more than sixty buildings - houses, barns and byres - thirteen tenants and a population approaching a hundred people. Bere, a coarse form of barley, oats and potatoes were growing in the fields and hundreds of cattle, horses, goats and sheep were grazed on the hillside above. By the 1820s the number of buildings in use had halved and today there is one tenant working on an upland livestock farm of sheep and cattle.

One of the settlements was called **Marik Gate** 837 654 and in the eighteenth century there were twenty buildings here on the site of what had been the Black Castle of Invervack. When the chief of Clan Donnachaidh lost his island fortress on Loch Tummel in 1513, he built a fortified tower house here which became the main residence of the clan chiefs until it was razed to the ground by Cromwellian troops in the 1650s. Robert Robertson, the 7th clan chief died in this tower house and it was said of him that he was:

> . . . good to those under him, did nothing unjustly and wronged no one. He was a blessing to all his own and was held in great esteem among his neighbours.

A solitary millstone in the ground, last remnant of the Milton of Invervack. The last reference to the mill appeared in 1823.

One of the Robertson of Struan corn mills was at **Muilean** (mill) 842 652 and it is marked on Timothy Pont's manuscript of 1600. All that remains now is part of a solitary millstone embedded in the ground and a walled enclosure once renowned for the quality of vegetables grown there. The last reference to the mill appeared in 1823 when Robert Douglas, the miller, was summoned to Perth court, accused of shooting deer illegally. In his defence he claimed that:

> . . . he and others had followed a hart at the end of December, chased from the hill by one of the Duke's deerhounds to the banks of the Garry. He had been accused of shooting it although he had no such intention and had not fired his gun.

Because of extreme poverty, Robert Douglas could not afford the cost of the journey to defend himself.

In 1695 an Invervack tenant called Alexander McGlashan accused James McCanich of stealing one of his sheep:

> In the month of September last bypast did wrongously intromit with and awaytake ane sheep pertaining the said personor and killed the same and upon searching and reaping the ground the said personor sheep was found in the defender House without head or skine. . .

McCanich admitted that he had found five or six sheep near his house, belonging to McGlashan and had shut them in his barn, intending to return them the next day but his herd unknowingly released them with his own flock and that morning:

> . . . certain honest neighbours who were searching and reaping the ground did find in the said defender his house a carkasse or bulk of a Ewe without head or skin which the said Defender killed . . . But alleged that the bulk found was his own, of a sheep he killed because it had the Sturdie and that he did thereafter cast away the head thereof in the River of Garry and sold the skin to ane merchand. . .

McCanich was found guilty and had to pay £2.6s 8d. plus 24 shillings expenses to McGlashan, and 'be committed to prison or taken be the Ground Officer to Custody' till the money was paid. He also had to pay £100 to the court and find a caution of 500 merks for his good behaviour.

Robert Ban (Fair Robert), father of Donald Robertson of Woodsheal, and a close kinsman of the chief, was the tenant of Milton of Invervack. Like most of that family, he was a fervent Jacobite supporter. In the autumn of 1746 a party of government troops, comprising a corporal and eight soldiers, crossed the Tummel Bridge on their way to Inverness and halted for a rest, placing their weapons against a large boulder behind them. They were thus observed by Rob Ban, who, alone and armed only with a gun, pistol and broadsword, nevertheless saw a chance of outwitting the redcoats. He positioned himself between the soldiers and their guns, took them by surprise by telling them they were surrounded and ordered them to surrender. Completely taken in by this, the soldiers gave in and allowed him to carry off all their weapons, not discovering the deception until both Rob Ban and the guns had completely disappeared.

Barony of Struan

Above Invervack the Tummelside track passes a large limestone quarry, once used by the local settlements, and then descends gently towards Loch Bhac. On a February night in 1437 King James I of Scotland was murdered in the royal apartments of the Blackfriars Monastery in Perth.

The perpetrators were Sir Robert Graham, a great grandson of Robert II; Walter Stewart, Earl of Atholl, uncle of the king and Walter's grandson,

The rocky overhang beside Allt Ghramaich where the murderers of James I were captured. Loch Bhac is in the background.

Sir Robert Stewart; Sir John Hall and his brother Thomas and the two brothers, Christopher and Thomas Chambers. The murderers fled to the hills and the first three hid near Loch Bhac where they were discovered and captured by Robert Riabhach or "grizzled" Robert Duncanson, chief of Clan Donnachaidh and a staunch supporter of the king. They were skulking under a large rock overhang on the bank of the small stream called **Allt Ghramaich** (Graham's Burn) which flows into the loch. The rock is there to this day and the burn takes it name from the ringleader, Sir Robert Graham.

It is pretty harrowing to read the accounts of the tortures to which the murderers were subjected. William Marshall in his *Historic Scenes of Perthshire* gives us a graphic account of the fate that befell the Earl of Atholl:

> The punishment of Walter, Earl of Atholl, was inflicted on three consecutive days. On the first day he was placed in a cart in which a stock-like engine was erected, and by ropes let through pulleys he was hoisted up on high; the ropes being suddenly let go, he fell down, but stopped near the ground, with intolerable pain by the luxation of the joints. Then he was set on a pillory that everyone might see him and a red-hot iron crown set on his head, with this inscription, "THE KING OF TRAITORS". On the second day he was bound upon a hurdle and drawn at a horse's tail through the principal streets of Edinburgh. On the last day, he was laid upon a plank, in a conspicuous place, his bowels were cut out while he was yet alive, and then thrown into the fire before his face; afterwards his heart was pulled out and cast into the same fire. His head was cut off, exposed to the view of all, and set on a pole in the highest part of the city. His body was divided into four quarters which were sent to be hung upon the most noted places of the principal cities of the Kingdom.

At the coming of age of James II in 1451, a royal charter granted the 'free Barony of Strowane for the love and favour His Majesty bore to Robert Duncanson for his apprehending the wicked traitor Robert Le Graham'. This is commemorated in the chief's coat of arms by a hand upholding a crown and also by the presence of a man in chains (representing Robert Graham) in the compartment underneath.

Standing Stones

About a mile east of Loch Bhac are the standing stones of **Na Carraigean** 839 620, in a clearing in a modern plantation, on the summit of **Meall na Clachan** (hill of stones) at a height of nearly 1,400 feet. They were known locally as **Na Clachan Aoraidh** (stones of worship) and are close to a small peaty loch called Lochan na Leathain. Before the trees were planted, they were on the most prominent part of a level crest of wide, rolling moorland from which no less than sixty separate and distinct summits, peaks, knolls and hills could be seen. Here in the distant past were erected four great squat and rough boulders, about ten feet apart and in the centre of a slightly raised mound, which was marked off from the moorland by a circle of smaller boulders and with an avenue roughly paved with smaller stones, leading to it. In more recent times there are accounts of the circle being visited at Beltane (1st May) and good fortune was supposed to come to those who walked round it.

About half a mile west of Invervack lies a small settlement called **Tombane** (white knoll) 829 653 from where in 1832, Alex Robertson was summoned to appear in the Dunkeld Court, accused by the Excise of smuggling malt which had been found in his kiln. Alex insisted that his neighbour, Donald Gow, had used his kiln without permission to dry his malt and would confess this in court.

The standing stones of Na Carraigean on top of Meall na Clachan.

The next settlement, **Pitaldonich** (share of the Sunday burn) 826 655 through its name, shows its connection with the nearby healing spring, reinforced by the adjoining house called **Tigh an Tobair** (well house). This spring was reputedly famous 'for curing all the ills that flesh is heir to', especially rheumatic ailments. People looking for a cure came to this spring on the first Sunday in May, and following the old pre-Christian tradition, would hang scraps of cloth and ribbon on the bushes as an offering, before bathing in the water. The story is told of a woman from Glen Fincastle, so crippled by rheumatism that she had to be wheeled the four miles over the hill, who was miraculously cured after her immersion in the spring, and able to walk home.

Boat of Pitaldonich, where the boat for the Bruar Ferry was moored, was located a few hundred yards upstream from the **Bruar Ford** 826 658, at a wide and level part of the Garry. Man has been crossing the river at this point for centuries and still continues to do so, as the bridge carrying the new A9 over the river is only a few yards away.

A track leads up the hill from Glebe Cottage and after a few hundred yards reaches the site of **Bee Jock's Croft** 832 663, at the edge of the trees. This was named after a John Robertson who lived there with his widowed mother, reclaimed the land and built a cottage in 1870. By the end of the century, the minister, the Rev. James Fraser, who held the lease for Bee Jock's Croft, described as Upper Baluain, was anxious to dispose of it and his letter to the estate factor reveals his dilemma:

> 14th June 1899
> My dear Mr Robertson
> Upper Baluan is a terrible bother to me at present . . . May I be allowed to tell these two men - most objectionable both as possible tenants of what wretched house - that His Grace is an offerer and that he shall have the first refusal? Common humanity and Christian neighbourhood forbid my disturbing the McIntoshes when poor Johnnie is just dying. My idea is to leave them there till November: then the place must cease to be a common lodging house and private asylum. There will be no "eviction" but I will be glad to know that the Duke with consent of the Presbytery, will buy or feu the place . . . The view is the very loveliest in Atholl. We shall not haggle about terms, be very sure of that.
> Yours very truly
> James Fraser.

There is no trace left today of **Calbruar** (Wood of Bruar) 828 661, a few hundred yards west of Baluain, though in 1900 it consisted of two double houses, thatched and in good order, beside the railway. Donald Stewart, a tenant there, was accused on 8 May 1713 of stealing a mare and a horse from the widow of William Murray in Blair, as written down in the Court records:

> . . . the said defender intromitted [interfered] with and away took a poor old mear belonging to the said William Murray and lugg marked the same . . . and wilfully refuses to give her back, and being so proven ought not only be decerned to give the said mear but also to pay fourty pounds Scots money as the price of a 3-year old staig [stallion] belonging to the said William Murray that was pasturing with the said mear at the time he took her away . . .

Several ploughmen testified against Donald Stewart and he eventually confessed to the crime. The Baillie of the court 'not only decerned the defender to give back the said mear but also to find out and deliver to the said Amelia Murray the 3-year old staig on or before the 1st June instant or to pay to her the said £40 Scots as his pryce . . .'

Calvine Tenants

Calvine Post Office in the late nineteenth century, now a private house. Calvine had a population of sixty six in 1823.

The village of **Calvine** 805 658 had a population of sixty six in 1823 which included a midwife, shoemaker, wheelwright, four weavers and also a grocer's shop.

A Calvine lady out for a Sunday afternoon stroll at the end of the last century.

In 1735 Alexander Robertson was summoned to the Baron Court to answer a complaint by Lady Faskally about the non-delivery of loads of peat to her residence and therefore not fulfilling his rental agreement. She complained that:

> . . . whereas some of them makes a custom of employing others to lead their peats in summer so that those are long in comeing to do the same but wait first to lead their own peats & thereafter when at leasure comes to lead hers so that her peats is ruined before this time and when they do come, but some this and some the next day by so doing her servants are kept from perfecting their work . . . and particularly upon Alexander Robertson in Calvein for not leading his peats this year at all . . . All ought to come on the same day and lead their peats as usuall as also lead their firr [firwood used as a candle] yearly . . . or to pay 9/- Scots for each lead [load] firr unlead . . .

In 1797 the Duke of Atholl received a petition confirming the good character of Donald Gow, a Calvine tenant, signed by:

> . . . no less than twelve of the most respectable tenants in his neighbourhood with whom he from the said certificate gives him the best of character and proves him a good neighbour.

Donald Gow had been accused by Donald McMillan of creating a disturbance on a Sunday morning. Gow maintained that it was McMillan who was 'the foundation of the vile complaint' and accused him of being involved in the 'late riot which happened in this place':

> . . . McMillan himself was the only contriver in gathering the mob in the west corner of this parish and upon the Sunday morning. Before day of light the ringleaders of the mob assembled in McMillan's house and gave them injunctions how to proceed in order to screen or save his son William from being Ballated as a militia man. That as soon as he upon the said Sabbath morning set the mob a going he himself went to Athole House [Blair Castle] to give himself credit and to put a good face upon his bad conduct & to accuse others and shelter himself.

The twelve tenants from Calvine, Shenval, Pittagowan and Bridge of Bruar signed a certificate, confirming that Donald Gow:

> . . . has been born and brought up in this neighbourhood from his infancy and that he always bore an honest character & unoffensive to his neighbours.

Impounded Cattle

The shooting lodge at **Clunes** (pasture) 782 671 was built in 1867, extended the following year and lies down the hill from the old settlement of the same name.

In 1802 a number of tenants petitioned the Duke about a Clunes tenant called William Stewart who kept impounding any cattle that strayed on to his pasture. They emphasised that they had tried to be good neighbours by returning any of his beasts found on their grazing, but he never reciprocated, always demanding payment while refusing to pay anything on account of his own strays. The factor described him as 'a very difficult person to deal with' when Stewart insisted that he had paid his debts for 1816 and could produce witnesses to prove it. The factor decided to confiscate his holding as quickly as possible to prevent him from removing his stock.

A house in the old settlement of Clunes. William Stewart, subject of a complaint by nearby tenants, lived here around 1800.

The old Clunes settlement lies astride the military road completed in 1729 and about half a mile distant on each side are two fine examples of Wade bridges, both restored in recent years through the Association for the Protection of Rural Scotland. The one to the east is called the **Window Bridge** 791 668 and crosses Allt a'Chrombaidh, while the one to the west crosses **Allt nan Cuinneag** 781 678, both forming links in this section of well-preserved Wade road.

The 'Window Bridge' near Clunes, on the military road from Perth to Inverness, was built in 1728 and restored a few years ago.

Wester Dalriach (brindled haugh) 761 693 is still used as a holiday home with a bench mark set in the wall.

Donald Robertson was the tenant farmer here and when he died in 1785, his widow, Janet MacDonald ran the farm. Her brother Angus felt sorry for her, so he moved in with her to help with the farm work and bring up the children. Two years later Janet obtained a fourteen-year lease and Angus began to improve the holding through building dykes and barns and converting the waste ground into arable land, all at his own expense. Imagine his astonishment, therefore, in 1797 when his sister 'executed a summonse of removing' against him which resulted in his being ejected from the farm. Janet was proposing to give up the running of the farm to her unmarried son who at that time was in service elsewhere.

The settlement of **Woodsheal** (speckled shieling) 775 669 appears on modern maps as Breac Ruidh and lies south of the Garry next to the also abandoned farms and green pastures of Achlany.

Woodsheal was the home of Donald Robertson, son of Robert Ban Robertson of Invervack. He led Clan Donnachaidh as a Captain in the Atholl Brigade under Lord George Murray at Culloden as the Poet Chief was by then too old and infirm to go into battle. He was wounded in the battle and left for dead, but survived and escaped to France. In 1764 he was living in Charleville in Champagne but the longing for his homeland was irresistible and on 17 April he wrote a heartfelt letter to the 3rd Duke:

> My Lord
> Though I have not the Honnour of being known to your Grace, I cannot help makeing bold to give this trouble to congratulate your Grace upon your being now at the head of what belongs to you by the Laws of God and man; and to assure your Grace that I pray God to bliss and preserve your Family.
>
> The Honnour done me by your Grace's forefathers encourages me to aske your protection, in order that I may breathe the aire of Atholl once more.
>
> I hope your Grace will give me a small farme that will yield milk and meal for my Little family. I refer my character to Abercairny, who I hope will promiss that I will pay the rent if I am able. . .

There is a happy ending to this plea, as Donald Robertson did return to Atholl, where he no doubt died a happier man, in 1775.

The land between **Dalnamein** (haugh of the mine) 753 695 and the Pass of Drumochter was feued by the 2nd Duke of Atholl in 1738 to Donald MacDonnell, who immediately assumed the title of 'Lochgarry'. He was accused of high treason for his involvement in the 1745 Jacobite uprising and banished abroad.

The estate contained a number of settlements with a great many tenants, who in 1755 were:

> . . . under great Dread of the Minister of Blair Atholl as he intends to put upon them a great proportion of his remuneration.

All tenants contributed to his stipend and this appeared as part of their rentals. However, the Lochgarry tenants maintained that as the estate originally was made up of shielings (places of summer pasture), they had never contributed to the stipend and failed to see why it should now be levied. The factor had a low opinion of the tenants, disparagingly calling them 'Dalnameiners' because they took little heed of his instructions and continued to use the runrig system of crop cultivation, much as their forefathers had done.

The wonderful set of drawings in Dalnamein Lodge featuring shooting scenes and characters at the turn of the century.

Fatherless Babes

A petition was lodged in 1776 by Alex McDonald, a resident in Edinburgh, on behalf of his nephews, Alex and James, and his niece, Isobel, who lived in Dalnamein. MacDonald's brother John, the father of the children, had recently died and his widow, Janet Gow, had remarried, a few weeks later, a much younger man, 'merely to hurt the said children', claimed Alexander. When he was said to have heard that Janet 'was planning to throw the children destitute', he applied on behalf of 'the poor fatherless Babes', to take over the lease of the farm in order to care for them.

The factor, Mr James Small, was not impressed as his sceptical comments show:

> The Petr. had a brother a tennant in Dalnamine - part of the estate of Lochgarrie. This man died lately and left a widow and children. The Petr. at Whitsunday last wanted to enter into his deceased Brother's farm which could not be done. And now under the Pretence of takeing better care of his Brother's children, than a Step Father will do, wants to get the farm at Whitsunday next. The factor is humbly of

A magnificent catch in the Garry at Dalnamein in 1921. Because of hydro-electric schemes there is very little water in the Garry now.

> oppinion that its a matter of indifference to the children which of the two possesses the farm as no doubt their share of the effects will be sold and security taken in their name from the Lover - The only question remaining is whether a Mother or an Uncle will take the most care of the Infant Children.

Dalinturuaine (haugh of rumbling stream) 759 691, lies across the Garry from Dalnamein and eight tenants possessed it in the eighteenth century.

It was suggested to the factor in 1763 that the steadings of two of the tenants be moved to the other end of Dalinturuaine as the settlement stretched out for over a mile along the bank of the river. This would be a help to one of the tenants, Duncan Robertson, Ground Officer and Constable:

> . . . he having frequent occasion to find Quarters and Carriages to His Majesties fforces when upon their march either South or North. Because the place proposed for the new steadings are half a mile nearer the King's Road [military road] than the present buildings are, and more contiguous to that part of the arable land which lyes there at such a distance, and cannot in the present situation manure or labour said ground to the satisfaction of any concerned. . .

Duncan Robertson was in agreement, as his petition shows:

> . . . As there is no Constable in the Neighbourhood, he has hitherto served all the Troops and others on His Majesty's Service with horses and such Carriages as the Country can afford, and is often oblidged to go along with such horses and carriages in order as much as he can to prevent disputes which often arise between the Tennants and the Troops. He is also oblidged to provide Fireing and Blanckets for the party stationed in the summertime at Dalnacardoch.

The factor confirmed that this would be an advantage as the cultivable ground was about a mile in length with the houses clustered at one end. His report continued:

> . . . to remove therefore two of the tenants (who are eight in number) to the other end would be a very great advantage to the farm, both as to Carriage of Dung, better labouring, and keeping of Corns; as Cattle often come from the Hill and destroy their Corns, as they lye at such distance from them and building the new houses as proposed would cost in ffactor's humble opinion about twelve Pounds Sterling. . . The ffarm of Dalinderuaine is but a very indifferent one, and the possessors all poor men.

The Harassed Widows

In 1797 trouble erupted among the tenants, when two widows, Christian Stewart, with six children and Rachel Cameron, with seven, complained that Donald Cameron:

> . . . instead of showing them good neighbourhood and affording them humanity, takes the opportunity at all times, to harass, beat, bruise and destroy them.

The widows became so desperate that they decided to 'lay him under a surety of lawburrows and to recover damages for injury and loss sustained'. Lawburrows was a process whereby a court could protect someone who believed they were in danger, by ordering another not to molest them. Later, more tenants complained about the conduct of Donald Cameron and his wife:

> They had chased their neighbours sheep with dogs over the water so that lambs were lost. They assaulted some of their neighbours and

> then had tried to blackmail others by threatening violence to sign a petition but by getting Cottars drunk, had prevailed on them to sign.
>
> They knocked one of the poor widows sons and his wife sighted a stone on the thigh of the other widows sons till he was lame for 3 weeks at harvest time.

Trouble flared up again in 1813 when Ewan Cameron complained that Donald Cameron's horses had strayed during the night and damaged his corn to the amount of ten threaves (a threave equalled 24 sheaves):

> The horses were caught and shut up . . . and denied to Donald till he paid for the damages. Donald Cameron threatened to lay his foot on Ewan's neck and went and broke the door of the barn.

All parties concerned were called to the Court in Dunkeld where they were given an order to 'flit' at Whitsunday, but were apparently allowed to stay, Donald and his family being 'utterly shaken off [by] the fear of God'.

The bad feelings and accusations rumbled on, with complaints of disturbance to animals and a case of dog stealing concerning a Pointer dog valued at £12, which was 'take away by warrant'. The complainers' roles were reversed in 1818 when Donald Cameron accused Ewan and his wife of being 'very bad neighbours':

> . . . They take my horses at night out of the hill and put them through injury. Their children forced our cows over the rocks at the east of our arable land, as ordered by their mother. They have cottars from Badenoch who abused with a bad tongue. Ewan's wife was seen taking some of their hay out of the barn and she was followed one snowy morning when tracks and traces of hay led to her byre.

Ewan sought redress through a petition to the Duke in which he claimed that he had had to resort to the Justices of the Peace who had granted a warrant for Donald and his family to keep the peace, but when they 'had defied the Constables of Court', Ewan and his family 'had gone in danger of their lives'. He asked that Donald Cameron and his family be removed, saying that he would be willing 'to take over their holding and remove from his own, rather than continue as at present'. In the end, both families were removed and this, in conjunction with all the other discord led to the factor's view that the Dalinturuaine tenants were 'a mischievious set of people, constantly thieving and fighting'.

Ruins of Tomicaldonich, home of Duncan Robertson, who suffered a financial loss at the hands of an Edinburgh lawyer.

The settlement adjoining Dalinturuaine to the north was called **Tomicaldonich** (knoll of the son of Duncan) 753 693 and living here in the eighteenth century was an old man called Duncan Robertson, who had loaned all his savings of 2,000 merks (£111 Sterling) to his landlord, Donald MacDonnell of Lochgarry, in 1738, when he bought the feu. When Duncan tried to get his money back in 1774, he learned that:

> . . . in the ranking of creditors of Lochgarry in place of his wadsett [loan] sum of £111, he was ranked only for £48.2s.8½d and, falling unhappily into the hands of a writer [lawyer] in Edinburgh, who preferred his own interests to that of the petitioner, over persuaded him that he would get him his whole money. . .

To Duncan's 'great surprise and mortification' the court threw out his case and his legal fees of £18 reduced his total to £30. By this time the factor had taken pity on him as his report demonstrates:

> The petitioner, far advanced in life has a wife and several young children yet unable to provide for themselves. If the Hon. Board in respect of the particular hardship of his case and calamatous situation would be humanely

> pleased to forgive the bygone claim of rent and to continue him in possession, that, with a small reversion of £30, would enable him to bring up his family, two of them may yet make good soldiers to His Majesty. Otherwise they must all go a begging . . . He is a poor old man who was mislead by a villian of a Writer. . . And to crown his misfortune he hapened to miss his way in the Walk of Leith one night, being a stranger and by a fall got his leg broke which must prove very hard upon him in his time of life.

Another three tenants, Alex McGlashan, James Robertson and Patrick Robertson, living in Tomicaldonich in 1799 fell out with their neighbour in the Dalnacardoch Inn, Patrick Robertson, the vintner. While they complained that he 'had been taking firr off their land after digging it up for use in his Pantries', he complained that their horses, cattle and sheep strayed on to his land, so he impounded them. The Tomicaldonich men maintained he had no right to do so, as 'there was no liberty of pounding without dykes', at which Patrick came across 'with a body of men carrying Black Dirks', threatening 'to cutt the horses threats [throats] or their lifes'.

As well as falling out with his neighbours, Patrick was constantly asking for repairs and complaining about expenses which he had incurred, driving the factor, Mr George Farquar to write to the Duke in exasperation in 1803:

> As if all the name of Robertson were inspired at once by the Demon of litigation that rascal at Dalnacardoch has issued summons for £300 damages for being kept out of possession for a year after he was by his bargain to enter as agreed.

Dalinriach (haugh of the heather) 729 699 was a small settlement beside the military road from Dalnacardoch to Aberfeldy, which crosses the Garry by **Drochaid Dail an Fhraoich** (bridge of the haugh of heather) 726 700. By 1800 its principal use was as a drove road to the trysts at Crieff and Stirling. There was a drove stance just south of the river, where livestock rested for the night and also a 'hospital' stance for sick animals.

Droving was causing problems to the Dalinriach tenants as is shown in their petition of 1758:

> Your Lordships will please know that the Town of Dalinrich lyes upon the High Road so as the Whole Droves traveling from the North to the South lay a night upon the Grasing of the said Town to the great hurt and prejudice of your Petitioners and which was not usuall until the whole neighbouring Heritors make the Drovers pay Grass Maill for their cattle.

The factor acknowledged that 'the Drovers are very hard on Dalinrich', and that 'most of the neighbouring heritors make the Drovers pay a small Gratuity for Grass'. He therefore left their rent as before and the additional amount asked for was 'to be struck out of the factor's charge'.

Glen Garry School

The disused **Glen Garry School** 733 702 still stands between the old and new A9 roads, less than a mile south of Dalnacardoch.

In 1777 the Rev. Duncan Stewart, a minister of Balquhidder and the Rev. Alex Small, minister of Kirkmichael, visited the school and made the following report:

> The Scholars make tolerable Proficiency in Reading, English, Writing, Spelling & Repeating the Catechism.

The disused Glengarry School near Dalnacardoch, now has had many of its slates removed.

In that year there were 20 pupils in the school: 12 boys and 8 girls. Four years later, an inspection of the Charity School at Dalnamein led to the observation that the schoolmaster 'teaches no Latin in his school. . . but is Faithful and Diligent in his Office'. The following table gives us an insight into the composition of pupils, their ages and teaching content in 1781:

	Boys' Names	Age	Entry	Began With	Progress
1.	Patrick Robertson	15	24 Oct	Bible	Writes & Compts.
2.	Patrick Gow	11	25 Oct	Bible	Bible, Writes & Compts.
3.	Don. McDonald	16	27 Oct	New Testament	Bible, Writes.
4.	Alex McDonald	11	23 Oct	" "	" "
5.	Jas. McDonald	10	23 Oct	" "	Bible
6.	Chas. Robertson	11	24 Oct	Proverbs	New Testament
7.	Angus Robertson	13	23 Nov	Bible	Bible, Writes & Compts.
8.	Alex McDonald	14	24 Nov	"	" " "
9.	Duncan Gow	14	24 Nov	"	" " "
10.	Don. Robertson	13	22 Nov	"	" " "
11.	John Robertson	7	8 Nov	Catechism	Proverbs.
12.	Chas. Robertson	7	2 Nov	"	"
13.	Alex. Robertson	10	6 Dec	"	"
	Girls' Names	**Age**	**Entry**	**Began With**	**Progress**
1.	Girsal Cameron	12	16 Oct	Bible	Bible & some other books.
2.	Marjory Robertson	12	16 Oct	"	" " " "
3.	Jean Cattanach	13	6 Dec	Proverbs	New Testament
4.	Elspet Robertson	11	16 Oct	"	" "
5.	Elspet McDonald	10	6 Dec	"	" "
6.	Chirstan McDonald	7	6 Dec	Catechism	Catechism
7.	Elspet Gow	7	6 Dec	"	"

9th March 1781

Two years later the Board for the Forfeited Estates had contacted Mr McLagan, surgeon at Taymouth with plans to carry out a smallpox inoculation scheme and his reply to Mr Menzies, the factor, in January 1783 was:

> . . . You are directed by the Board to pay half a crown each for inoculating the Children on the annexed Estates of Strowan & Loch Gary. They surely as not know that the medicines necessary for preparing them & during the continuance of the disease - and after the worst is over would very nearly come to the sum they offer. They should be likewise informed that some parts of the Estates are twenty miles from this place & as many miles from the one end to the other.
>
> I shall be obliged to you to inform them of this, as a proper excuse from me not accepting their offer. I am really sorry that from the smallness of the sum I am hindered from doing an action that I think so humane and proper - for I am informed that the smallpox is just now carrying of[f] one half of those that are sicked with it in that country. . . The current allowance in this country which you know is five shillings each and payment for the medicines.

Dalnacardoch Inn

The change-house or inn at **Dalnacardoch** (haugh of the smithy) 721 703 sat at an important junction on the military road network where the Perth to Inverness road met the road from Stirling and Aberfeldy. Here it was that Wade had his 'hutt' or headquarters when he was supervising this section of the road and was the forerunner to the inn, built in 1732 as a change-house on the 'King's Road'.

In 1757 the proprietor, John Macpherson, complained that:

> The House Stable and Kitchen at Dalnacardoch are in very bad repair, which gives great disgust

Dalnacardoch at the turn of the century. The wooden plaque can be seen to the right of the front porch.

> to travellers, that the Garden Wall is quite down which is a very great loss and is an inconvenience for travellers as they cannot be accommodated with Roots and Greens.

The Rev. Francis Gastrell toured the Highlands in 1760 and confirmed this when he wrote that the inn was so filthy that rather than dine there, his party sat outside on a green bank and ate ham, cheese and bread. The factor agreed that things should be better, saying in 1763:

> This is a stage no traveller on that road can avoid and that travellers do expect not only to be well used but to have things in a better and neater way. . . .

The factor went on to observe that the landlord was not well suited for the job as both he and his wife 'have never been bred but in the country way'. It was therefore decided to remove the landlord 'on account of bad entertainment to Passengers and neglect of his business' in 1764 and the tenancy was taken up by Donald MacDonald.

Meantime there was little in the way of improvement in conditions until 1774 when it was modernised and enlarged to ten bedrooms:

> . . . upon a much larger and more elegant plan than was the former, nay more so than any other Inn on that road.

In 1775 MacDonald's Widow, Elizabeth Fraser said she could not afford to buy furniture for the new inn and was rendered even less able to do so because:

> The Petitioner's stable having been fancied too narrow for the Horses that came there on 15 October last, the Servant of a Noble Lady [Lady Galloway] then in the house put her Ladyship's horses into the Old Kitchen then containing several pieces of furniture that had been in the Old House and the principall part of the kitchen furniture and by some unknown misfortune the said Kitchen, Brewhouse and the family room adjoining thereto were totally burnt to the Ground whereby the said Petitioner sustained a loss of £59 Ster estimating t

he value of the horses for which she never received any consideration from the Board.

In response, Mr Small, the factor was certain that:

> It is a fact that by the carelessness of Lady Galloway's Servants that kitchen, the Rooms and a good Brewhouse were burnt to the ground. . . he knows the want of a Brewhouse is both hurtfull and inconvenient to the Petitioner.

There is an interesting Bill of Fare for October 1776 when the farms were being valued for the Forfeited Estates by Mr Small:

Oct					
5th	To	10 Gentlemen including four Valuators at Dinner @ 8d each	£0	6	8
	"	10 Ditto at Supper	0	6	8
	"	2 bottles Port	0	5	0
	"	Punch	0	12	6
	"	7 Bottles Porter	0	3	6
	"	15 Bottles Ale	0	2	6
6th	"	Breakfast for 9 Gentlemen	0	6	0
	"	Dinner for 7 Gentlemen	0	4	8
	"	Supper for 7 Gentlemen	0	4	8
	"	2 bottles Port	0	5	0
	"	Punch	0	7	6
	"	3 bottles porter	0	1	6
	"	3 bottles Ale	0	0	6
	"	Brandy	0	2	0
	"	Whisky	0	0	8
7th	"	Breakfast for 7 Gentlemen	0	4	8
	"	Dinner for 3 Gentlemen	0	2	0
	"	Punch	0	2	6
	"	3 bottles Ale	0	0	6
	"	Brandy	0	2	4
	"	Supper	0	2	0
	"	Punch	0	2	6
	"	Servants ground officers eating and drinking for the above 3 days	0	12	0
	"	Corn and Hay for 8 horses for 3 nights	0	11	6
	"	Whiskey for tennants and Baillies	0	7	6
8th	"	Five feeds of corn	0	1	8
	"	Breakfast and Brandy	0	2	4
	"	Servants	0	5	0
			£6	5	10

After modernisation, standards at the inn improved as is shown by Henry Skinner's remarks after a night's stay in 1795, describing it as 'the good inn of Dalnacardoch, another of the houses erected by the Government'. Likewise William Larkin stated in 1818 that 'The inn at Dalnacardoch, like all those on this great thoroughfare is provided with all the accommodation that can reasonably be required'. The arrival of the railway line from Perth to Inverness in 1863 caused much of the traffic to be diverted away from the road and Dalnacardoch closed as an inn in 1865. However there is still a reminder of its past existence through a plaque on the wall above the front door which has the simple inscription 'Rest a little while A D 1774' in English, Latin and Gaelic.

Edendon Toll

The **Edendon Toll** 715 707, taken down during the A9 reconstruction work in the 1970s, lay half a mile to the north. A decision to levy tolls both here and at the County March, was taken in 1820 as a means of paying for the upkeep of the road. Tolls were levied on all passing traffic except foot travellers:

Carriages drawn by two horses	2/–
Gigs	9d
Saddle horses	3d
Carriers for hire	1/–

The Edendon Toll beside the recently-surfaced A9 in 1930.

Drovers were charged 5d per score of cattle and 2d for twenty sheep. This perhaps explains why the drovers began taking their beasts into Atholl over the Minigaig Pass route (see page 108) as it was a means of evading the tolls.

The Wade Stone in its original position beside the military road.

The **Wade Stone** 692 717 is about two miles further north and was erected in 1729 to commemorate the completion of the military road between Perth and Inverness. Tradition has it that Wade placed a guinea on top of the eight-foot stone and on his return a year later, found it still there. When the A9 was rebuilt in the 1970s the stone was taken down for safety and replaced in its original position, now beside the southbound carriageway, but less conspicuous against a background of heather, bracken and rocks.

Oxbridge

The bridge on the old A9 at Dalnaspidal replaced the **Oxbridge** 647 735, a few hundred yards upstream in the 1820s. This was the location of a great feast in 1729 to celebrate the completion of the road. Writing about this event on 2 October, Wade mentions travelling in his coach with great ease and pleasure:

> . . . to the feast of oxen which the Highwaymen [road builders] had prepared for us opposite Loch Garry, where we found four roasting at the same time in great order and solemnity. We dined in a tent pitched for that purpose; the beef was excellent and we had plenty of Bumpers [toasts] and after three hours stay took our leave of our benefactors the Highwaymen and arrived at the "Hutt" before it was dark.

This bridge near Dalnaspidal was built in the 1820s, replacing the original Oxbridge, a few hundred yards upstream.

When the military road was finished, the people of **Dalnaspidal** (haugh of the hospice) 645 731 saw opportunities to be gained from the passing traffic. Duncan Robertson converted his bothy into a public house and allowed drovers to rest their cattle on his pasture, provided they paid for it. Many travellers passed this way, including Queen Victoria in 1861, who recorded in her diary:

> . . . A little further on we came to Loch Garry which is very beautiful. . . There is a small shooting lodge or farm charmingly situated. . . We passed many drovers, without their herds and flocks, returning, Grant told us, from Falkirk.

The small shooting lodge noted by Queen Victoria was replaced earlier this century by a much larger building.

Loch Garry Battle

Loch Garry is quite a small loch, three miles long and is a reservoir for hydro-electricity, water being pumped through a huge underground tunnel to Loch Errochty. In the middle of the seventeenth century a battle took place here between a royalist army led by Lieutenant General Middleton, with 1,200 foot soldiers supported by 800 cavalry who had marched over from Rannoch, against a body of Cromwellian troops led by Colonel Morgan, who had progressed south from Ruthven. As the royalists retreated along the narrow defile beside Loch Garry, the cavalry became separated from the foot soldiers and were routed by the English troops. Many of the royalists escaped by dismounting and taking to their heels, but the English gained a rich prize of over 300 horses. This clash hardly ranks as a great set-piece engagement, yet its effect on the royalist cause was disastrous, as it seriously weakened their cavalry strength.

The Drumochter Pass in 1924, four years before the road was surfaced for the first time.

Nowadays the lochside is the setting for a more peaceful, yet perhaps far-reaching experiment. Set up some years ago under the inspiration of Ron Greer, the Loch Garry Tree Group has been planting native broad-leaved trees in the barren, deserted upland in an effort not only to show that trees can grow there and improve the quality of the environment, but also that leaf litter from the trees can enrich the food value in the loch and encourage fish life to thrive.

Just north of Loch Garry we enter **Drumochter** (summit ridge) 632 760 the great pass through the Grampians, described in an 1843 guide book as:

> The black and moorish wilds where nought but stunted grass and heather, dark swamp, impetuous torrents, grey rocks and frowning heights and precipices are to be seen. The mountains also are heavy and seem to be broken into great detached mounds.

Two of these mountains are **Meall an Dobharcain** (Sow 'of Atholl') 625 742 guardian of Atholl and **An Torc** (Boar 'of Badenoch') 621 763, protector of Badenoch.

Drumochter Fairies

At one time there was an old, stooped and one-eyed man whose horse was in an equally bad way, living in Lochaber. He was travelling from Loch Laggan with a cartload of herrings and stopped for the night on Drumochter, where 'sitheans' or fairy knolls abound. He strayed a little way off the road to a grassy bank, unyoked the horse and settled down for the night. When it was dark, he heard music coming from the hills and the words 'Monday' and 'Tuesday' . Having a good ear for music, he sang out 'Wednesday' to the same simple tune. At this, the fairies appeared, corrected his stoop, replaced his eye and cured his horse. Next morning this happy man drove on to Blair Atholl, sold all his herrings and when he got home, his wife failed to recognise him.

His neighbour, who was in a similar physical state, saw what had happened, so he got a load of herrings and set off for Blair Atholl also. He camped on the same grassy bank and was cured in the same miraculous fashion.

Coire Dhomhain (deep corrie) 630 753 is close to the county march and here in the eighteenth century up to a thousand head of cattle were to be found grazing in the summer months. At one time the march between Perthshire and Inverness-shire was marked by a number of boundary stones. One of these was known as the 'Chair Stone', where an ancient ritual took place. The stone, which resembled a chair, had charcoal placed beneath it, several witnesses were called on to testify to the boundary and had their faces blackened and slapped before being sworn to the march on bended, bare knees. Apparently the Chair Stone was demolished during the building of the military road in 1729. Other marked stones with 'A' for Atholl and 'B' for Badenoch marked the boundary, and one of these stood in such a way that:

> If you were to empty a pail of water on top, part of it would run to the County of Inverness and part of it to the County of Perth.

A toll bar was built here in 1821 and in 1830 it was recommended that a licence be granted 'to retail spirits and ale', no doubt fairly essential in this bleak and windswept place, even in summer.

Vision

The Sow of Atholl and the Badenoch Boar,
With litter of young hills about their sides,
Sleep in the shadow of the Sgairneach Mor.
Washing the glen of Edendon, the tides
Of light lap Gaick in a sunshine sea.
All in her christened colour Dearg lies,
While storm-dogs crowd
'Mid Beinn a' Ghlo's peak-welter to crash free,
Slavering and howling black across the skies,
And tear the throat from the white hind of cloud.

J B Salmond

Aerial view of Glen Garry from the north.

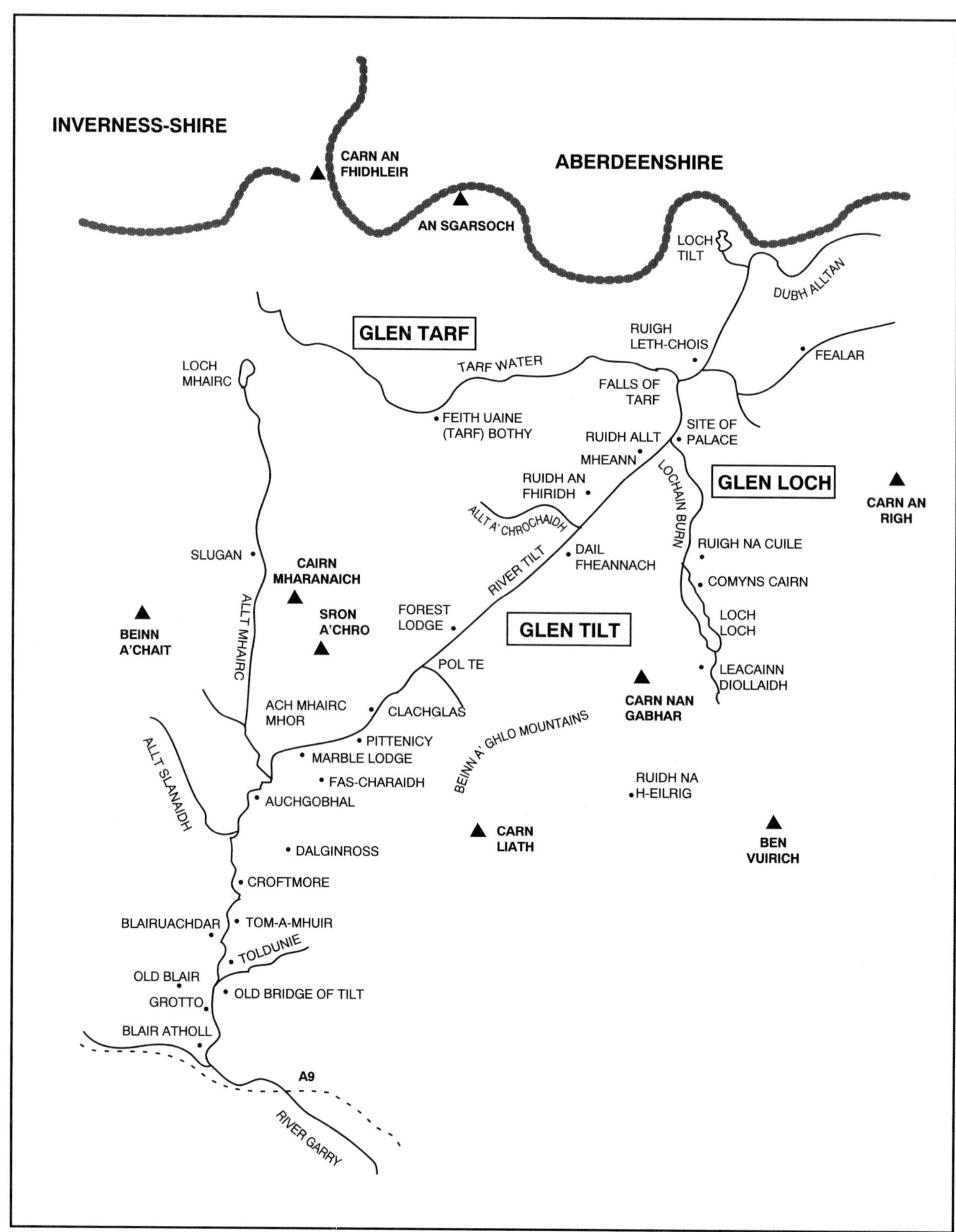
INVERNESS-SHIRE
CARN AN FHIDHLEIR
ABERDEENSHIRE
AN SGARSOCH
LOCH TILT
DUBH ALLTAN
GLEN TARF
RUIGH LETH-CHOIS
FEALAR
LOCH MHAIRC
TARF WATER
FALLS OF TARF
FEITH UAINE (TARF) BOTHY
RUIDH ALLT MHEANN
SITE OF PALACE
GLEN LOCH
CARN AN RIGH
RUIDH AN FHIRIDH
LOCHAIN BURN
ALLT A' CHROCHAIDH
SLUGAN
CAIRN MHARANAICH
DAIL FHEANNACH
RIVER TILT
RUIGH NA CUILE
COMYNS CAIRN
BEINN A'CHAIT
ALLT MHAIRC
SRON A'CHRO
FOREST LODGE
GLEN TILT
LOCH LOCH
POL TE
LEACAINN DIOLLAIDH
CARN NAN GABHAR
ACH MHAIRC MHOR
CLACHGLAS
BEINN A' GHLO MOUNTAINS
PITTENICY
ALLT SLANAIDH
MARBLE LODGE
FAS-CHARAIDH
RUIDH NA H-EILRIG
AUCHGOBHAL
CARN LIATH
BEN VUIRICH
DALGINROSS
CROFTMORE
BLAIRUACHDAR
TOM-A-MHUIR
TOLDUNIE
OLD BLAIR
GROTTO
OLD BRIDGE OF TILT
BLAIR ATHOLL
A9
RIVER GARRY

CHAPTER THREE

GLEN TILT & GLEN TARF

Glen Tilt is sixteen miles in length from its meeting with Glen Garry at Blair Atholl, to the Perthshire/ Aberdeenshire watershed. It is a beautiful glen, steeped in history, with evidence of man's endeavours everywhere to be seen.

The glen has changed little in over 200 years except in one vital respect - people. Now there are fewer than ten people living there on a permanent basis, but over 200 years ago, there were hundreds, of all ages, living out their lives, working on the land and at the shielings, raising their children, but all that remains are the sad footing and ruins of their homes, everywhere to be seen.

In 1838 the Blair Atholl minister, the Rev. John Stewart, tried to account for the continuing decline of the glen population and wrote:

> In former times, the high grounds were inhabited by numerous tenants. Their possessions were small and their supply of farinaceous foods precarious and in the best season offered only a scanty subsistence. They had no potatoes and their principal aliment was animal food. A system of more beneficial management had converted these dreary and comfortless habitations into sheep-walks.

A general view of Glen Tilt which was formed by glaciation.

William Scrope, the famous nineteenth century sportsman spent many hours deer stalking in Glen Tilt and described the scene:

> Salmon came up the Tilt in full waters, and are taken with the fly; and all the other rivers are so full of small trout, that any one who pleases may catch as many dozens in a day as he can conveniently carry. These streams work their way in solitude through dreary mosses, and come winding down the glens sometimes in comparative tranquillity, and at others bursting and rooting up every thing about them; the mighty force with which they descend may be read in the vast rocks and fragments of wreck which they heap up as monuments of their power. Supplied by such numerous forces, the Tilt becomes powerful in its infancy. Born in rugged regions, it cleaves its way, at the base of impending mountains and rocky precipices, in a dark, deep and narrow trench. Arrived at the green pastures of Ben-y-gloe, its bed begins to expand, and the waters pass down in freer course; still however they come racing and flashing along with overwhelming violence.

Until the start of the eighteenth century, ownership of the glen was split between Atholl on the west side and Lude to the east, as seen in General Robertson of Lude's 1790 manuscript:

> A cow may drink in the River Garry at Invertilt from which she may go on the land of the Laird of Lude without crossing another man's, until she crosses the ford of Dail a' Chruineachd at the head of Glen Tilt.

Right of Way Case

The right of way to Deeside starts on the east side of the glen and to quote from the famous court case, establishing it as such, in the middle of the last century:

> . . . From time immemorial there has been a public road communicating between the villages of Castletown of Braemar and the village of Blair Atholl.

A* Punch *cartoon showing one of the botanists contemptuously cocking a snook at two kilted ghillies, as they made their escape from Glen Tilt, which, as a result, led to the right of way case.

The case arose from an incident on Saturday 21 August 1847, when a party of six botanists, Messrs Douglas, Gilby, Hewetson, Ivory, Morse and Murchison, led by Professor Balfour set out from Braemar to walk through the glen, studying its flora, believing the road to be a public one. After proceeding for eight or nine miles, they encountered a shooting party somewhere near Clachglas. This party consisted of Captain Oswald of Dunnikier, Captain Drummond of Megginch and six attendants with dogs and guns. The botanists were challenged for walking on a private road and ordered to return to Braemar, which they politely, but firmly, refused to do, saying they were unaware they were trespassing.

They continued down the glen, at last encountering a padlocked gate at Tibby's Lodge, the old entrance from Atholl to the glen, where a ghillie told them they could not pass without the Duke's permission. *The Scotsman* of 1 September 1847 then took up the story:

> The Duke then said, "Well you must return; you don't move an inch further, unless you break open the gate, which you may do, and take the consequences. Don't spoil my walks with stamping. Come off that walk every one of you. Every step you take there is a trespass - a new trespass. I shall not count it an additional trespass if you return on the main Walk." Professor - "Oh, it's a trespass then on the side walk, but not on the main walk." The Duke - "I shall not waste any more words with you; you must return."

Under any circumstances, to return the same distance was out of the question, and the party refused to obey. According to *The Times* of 7 September, 'in their desperation, they made their escape over a wall, hotly pursued by the Duke's familiars.'

The case was then taken up by Alex Torrie, advocate; Robert Cox, Writer to the Signet and Charles Law a merchant. This powerful trio alleged that the road had been metalled in 1760, when it was placed under the control of the Commissioners of Supply in the County of Perth and was kept in repair by statute labour. The case came before the law in 1850 when the decision went against the Duke, who, refusing to give in easily, took it to the House of Lords, where he again lost and this decision led to the formation of the Scottish Rights of Way Society.

The Grotto 876 663 was part of the great garden landscaping in the eighteenth century and described by Robert Heron, another early traveller in 1793:

The Grotto with Queen Victoria and Lady Glenlyon admiring the view of the Tilt in 1844. Robert Heron described the scene in 1793.

> I was carried by my conductor by paths, the line of which I recollect not, to a grotto, in front of which poured a cataract. Within this grotto was a mossy seat - a scene where a hermit might forget the world and indulge in undisturbed meditation on the wonders of nature. Spars, several types of quartz disposed with some ores are disposed through the rude walls: from the roof hang stalactites.

The cataract seen by Heron is called the York Cascade after Drummond, Archbishop of York and was formed by the overspill from the lade of the old mills in Bridge of Tilt, as it plunged 50 feet into the Tilt.

Old Bridge of Tilt in 1860 when it contained eight houses and a population of twenty six. By 1870 the row of cottages had been replaced by a two-storey house.

Witches' Rock

Downstream is the **Witches' Rock** 875 662 which overhangs **Pol nam Ban** (pool of the women). Traditionally this is where adultresses were stitched up in sacks, thrown from the rock into the pool below and left to drown

The Witches' Rock in Glen Tilt in the last century. Adultresses were thrown in sacks from the top into the river below and left to drown.

Old Bridge of Tilt formerly Bridge of Tilt 876 664, before the military road was rerouted to its present line, contained eight houses and a population of twenty six, including a wool weaver, two saw millers and a grocer. Earlier there had been an inn, an attractive thatched cottage, on the right of the road, on the site where the old sawmill now stands. When the new road was built in the 1820s, McInroy of Lude built a new inn for £1,400 near the new bridge and we know it today as the Tilt Hotel.

Among the four local water mills, one was for processing flax, which is now Atholl Bank Cottage. In 1770 a case of theft arose here, with Donald Stewart the chief suspect. When John Gow came from Blairuachdar to collect his processed flax, half of it was missing. When Donald's house was searched, 'two parcels' were found at the foot of his bed, put there, according to his wife, by her father. Donald pleaded guilty and left the district, promising not to return for seven years. On the laird's instructions, eight pounds of lint were given to the poor.

The former lint mill, now Atholl Bank Cottage above Old Bridge of Tilt. A theft took place here in 1770.

Toldunie Oxen

Toldunie 878 668 was at one time a fertile farm with cottages, parks and an orchard. The name means 'hole of the men' and there is an old story that says one day the men were working in the fields when the ground opened up and swallowed them, to reappear across the river in a place called **Toldamh** (hole of the ox) 874 667, as oxen.

Tibby's Lodge in 1810, at the gateway to Glen Tilt, was pulled down in 1884. (Sketch by Lady Emily Murray)

Tibby's Lodge was built by the 2nd Duke of Atholl when the Wade road was constructed, at the main entrance to Glen Tilt. It got its name from Tibby Cameron, the gatekeeper who died in 1858. By the 1880s it was falling into disrepair and was taken down in 1884, being replaced by East Lodge, across the road.

Mrs Forbes, gatekeeper at Tibby's Lodge, with her spinning wheel in 1860.

MacIntosh's Rock

The MacIntoshes were thanes (Gaelic, Toiseach, meaning leader) of Glen Tilt until 1502 and their stronghold was on the east bank at **Tom-a-Mhuir**

877 670, a steep knoll on which there was still a substantial ruin until well into the last century. **Creag Mhic an Toisiche** (MacIntosh's Rock) 881 690 lies in the middle of the river above the Cumhann-leum Bridge. It was a tradition that the thane sat on this rock to hold his court, his people standing round to hear him mete out justice. On each occasion the court met, a man was apparently executed, but mercifully he could only hold court when the water was very low and he could reach the stone without getting his feet wet. This gave rise to the saying: 'It is not every day that MacIntosh holds his court.'

The estate road from Blairuachdar on the west bank crosses **Allt Slanaidh** (healing stream) 881 699 by a fine single-arch stone bridge built in 1759. This stream rises several miles distant on the south slopes of **Beinn a'Chait** (hill of the cat) 865 749. At its source there are two mineral springs, both called Duke James's Well after the 2nd Duke, which give rise to the name of the stream because of their healing properties.

The next bridge of note is Gilbert's Bridge, taking its name from an Atholl hillman, William Gilbert Stewart, whose cottage was nearby. One of the cottage walls is reputed to have held a striking set of drawings and its other claim to fame was through a later inhabitant, Elly Campbell, who was renowned for spreading butter with her thumb!

In March 1834, Lord Glenlyon's son, George, who succeeded his uncle to become the 6th Duke, had a serious accident on the hill face above **Ach Mhairc Mhoir** 888 716. When returning after a fox hunt with Peter Fraser, the stalker, they set fire to some heather, but it was slow to start, and to make it burn faster, George unwisely threw some gunpowder from his flask on to it but it exploded, severely injuring his right hand. Twenty years later, Peter Fraser's successor, Alex McAra, found the remains of the flask that had caused the damage all those years before.

Peter Fraser spent all his life in Glen Tilt, living in **Clachglas** (grey stone) 916 726 where his old home still stands near to the modern house occupied by today's keeper. Peter began working for the Atholl family as a young man and by 1839 was appointed as head stalker. When Victoria and Albert visited the glen in 1844, he often acted as guide, the Queen describing him as 'a wonderfully active man'. He is reported to have

Peter Fraser, head stalker, in Forest Lodge at the time of Queen Victoria's visit in 1844.

'Old Peter Fraser, former head Keeper there, now walking with the aid of two sticks'. Queen Victoria 1861.

complimented Albert on his shooting, saying he had been 'thirty seven years here and during that time I have not seen before so good a shot as you are'. It seems that Peter was something of a diplomat, as by all accounts, the Prince was not a very great shot. He held the position of head stalker until 1847 when he retired through being disabled with rheumatism and when the Queen met him again in 1861 she described him as: 'old Peter Fraser, former head keeper there, now walking with the aid of two sticks'.

The shieling, or summer pasture for Ach Mhairc Mhoir was three miles distant at the head of Gleann Mhairc. It was called **Slugan** (neck of a bottle) 887 751, where the remains of several bothies, one of them substantial, can still be seen on the west bank of the river.

Great Rock Fall

During the month of April in 1772 there was a remarkable rock fall near the shieling, which was noted down by John Crerar, an Atholl hillman, who was described by William Scrope as:

> The King of Sportsmen and good fellows... He was honest, faithful and most attached adherent of astonishingly active powers and possessed of admirable skill in stalking and shooting the deer, always selecting the finest hart. He was also a composer of music and many a fine dance have the lads and lasses had to the sound of my old friend's violin.

He had shown early signs of musical ability and became a pupil of the celebrated fiddler to the

Gleann Mhairc with the 'New Bridge' in the foreground. The spectacular rock fall took place at the head of this glen in 1772.

dukes, Niel Gow, afterwards composing many reels and airs.

His account of the rock fall is as follows:

> A considerable time before this singular event happened the weather was delightful in the extreme. However, two or three days before it happened the weather took a sudden change with an awful storm of snow so that the shepherds could not for a time, go to the hill with the sheep. When the hill was again considered pasturable, it was discovered by the shepherds that several large stones were removed out of the place in which they were before the storm commenced. They were scattered in every direction. Such was the power with which they were removed that several large stones which no number of men could move were thrown the distance of thirty and forty yards, even against the steep face of the hill.
>
> There were several causes assigned for this singular event, some thought they were removed by the falling heap of snow, others that they were removed by an extraordinary gust of wind, but the most probable opinion is that a shock of earthquake was the cause . . .
>
> The removal of these stones caused a great excitement in the country. They were visited during the ensuing summer by a great number, all ranks of people.

Donald Stewart was an eye-witness to this amazing event, as he was at the time staying in one of the bothies, and his account, taken down forty seven years later, when he was 71, elaborates on John Crerar's description:

> At the time there was fine weather in the spring till about the end of March, then came a dreadful storm of snow and wind. About a gunshot north of the house, on the north side of the burn that runs through the glen was and is a small knoll or hillock. On the north side of this hillock there was and is a moss. Great lumps of the moss were suddenly scooped out of the moss, and rolled along scattered by the whirlwind. A number of stones some of them very large size

> and weight were driven up the hill on the south side of the valley a considerable distance. The pits or holes made as they bounded were long visible and maybe visible yet for aught I know. There was one of them square and small pieces were broken off it. Another large stone that was standing near where they stood, was uplit and tumbled apiece down the knoll.

When questioned further, Donald answered that:

> There was a great many stones thrown across the burn but did not know the number. One of the largest stones he could not reach the top of with his hands when standing on the ground. This stone appeared to have been dragged for about 40 yards and not turned over. Many others were tons in weight.

This remarkable fall caused great excitement and wonder, bringing even the Duke himself, who pitched a tent nearby where he lunched with his family who had come especially to view the phenomenon. Some said it had been caused by an earthquake, others by an avalanche or even an extraordinary gust of wind. It is quite clear from whence the rocks had come. At this point the sides of the glen are very steep and near the top and level with the boulders, there is a jagged scar, obviously the origin of the substantial rockfall. The storm provided impetus to trigger the rockfall, descending boulders picking up enormous momentum as they rolled down the steep slope.

Cairn Mharanaich (Braemar cairns) 894 742 is a 2,600 feet (800m) mountain on the east side of Gleann Mhairc. Its name relates to a number of cairns, sixteen in all, raised by the men of Atholl to commemorate a victory they achieved over a marauding band of Braemar men who were returning home with their plunder when they were overtaken and sixteen of their number killed. Eight of the cairns were on the top of the mountain and the remainder a short way lower down on the south side. Very little is known about this skirmish and even its date is unknown.

First Powered Flight

Dalginross (haugh of the headland) 885 695 is on the edge of a wide upland grass plateau, several hundred feet above the glen floor, where one of the first powered aeroplanes was tested in the utmost secrecy. During the late summer of 1907 trials took place of an aeroplane invented and designed by John William Dunne but as it had only a 15 horsepower engine, it failed to take off. This activity was known locally as 'the mystery of the moors' and various members of the duke's staff were posted round, to keep away the locals and newspaper reporters. Further trials took place the following year and the first powered flight in Scotland, over a distance of a hundred yards, was achieved by Lieutenant Gibbs in October, with a more powerful engine. Despite this success, the official funding money ran out, so the Blair Atholl Aeroplane Syndicate was formed, with a share capital of £3,750 to further its development. On 10 December 1909 Articles of Association were signed by John George Murray, Lord Tullibardine; John Dunne and two engineers Capper and Carden. This enabled a successful aeroplane with a 50 horsepower engine to be developed elsewhere.

The peat road which terminates at **Moine Mor** (great moss) 903 709, formed part of the boundary of the Commonty, or common pasture which covered a long stretch of moorland between Glen Tilt and Glen Fender. Because of the remoteness and diversity of the boundary, it gave rise to many disputes among the tenants. Both the Duke of Atholl and Robertson of Lude claimed shooting rights over this ground and it was alleged by Atholl, that Lude, in order to annoy the Duke, encouraged his tenants to poach game, quietly undertaking to pay their fines if they were caught! Relations between the two estates worsened in 1803 when General William Robertson succeeded to Lude, as he was said at times to have taken a cannon on to the commonty march and fired it, thus scaring the deer on the other side of Glen Tilt and spoiling the Duke's sport. It was also alleged that he sometimes fired a cannon at deer grazing on the common pasture, with three 5-pound cannon balls being found later on the hill by some of the tenants and which are now kept in Blair Castle. **Caisteal Dubh** (black castle) 905 713 overlooks the old peat moss and has a commanding view of Glen Tilt to the north east. This was a dun or ring fort and faint traces of a circular turf bank are still visible below the summit.

Auchgobhal, opposite the Birkenburn, was the location for the glen school from 1776 to 1788.

Auchgobhal School

Auchgobhal (field of the fork) 885 706 is situated across the river from Ach Mhairc Mhoir and was a 42-acre farm.

On 7th May 1776, the Scottish Society for the Propagation of Christian Knowledge (SSPCK) opened a school here under the charge of Duncan Ferguson. He was paid £10 a year and taught forty boys and thirteen girls. He was plainly unhappy with his sub-standard accommodation, as he threatened to leave the next year - however he stayed on for another eleven years, during which time the roll peaked at fifty six in 1781, dropping to forty six in 1783 and forty four in 1786. By the next year, the Dunkeld Presbytery felt that numbers were insufficient to merit carrying on, so the school was closed, with Ferguson being moved to a school at Orchilmore, near Killiecrankie.

Evidence of the growing of lint (flax) is to be found a few hundred yards up the track where there are the visible remains of two lint pools. This is where sheaves of flax were immersed and left to 'ret' for ten to fourteen days, when the hard outer shell could be more easily removed, leaving the pithy core which was then further processed and turned into linen yarn.

Sheep shearing on the haugh land in front of Auchgobhal in 1860.

On the level ground beside the river, the tenants at one time grew their crops, but with the coming of sheep, by the 1850s it was the gathering place for hundreds of sheep and their handlers for the summer clippings.

The **Queen's Well** 890 710 issues from the rock face on the right of the road, opposite the

John Stewart, alias 'Black Jock', who lost a boot while leaping the river to win a bet.

confluence of Allt Mhairc and the Tilt. Apparently Queen Victoria was so taken with the purity and quality of its water, that a footman was sent every morning during her 1844 visit, to fill a bottle for her own personal use.

A little further on, where the river is narrower, is the site of **Leum nan Brog** (leap of the boot) 890 712. This is where John Stewart, alias 'Black Jock' lost a boot whilst leaping across the river to win a wager.

Marble Quarry

Marble Lodge 898 717 was built in 1815 as a small shooting lodge and is named after the nearby marble quarry, where work had recently begun to exploit it. **The marble quarry** 903 718 is on the east bank of the river and vestiges of the track to it can be seen beside Gow's Bridge. William Scrope described it in the 1820s:

> The whole of this glen, in a scientific point of view, is interesting in the highest degree; to a geologist there is none more so throughout Scotland. A quarry has been opened above Marble Lodge, which contains immense blocks of marble, varying from grass green into one of

Marble Lodge, built as a small shooting lodge in 1815, was named after the nearby quarry.

A clipping table and two characters at Auchgobhal.

a yellower cast, and intermixed with grey. The best blocks take a good polish; and they surpass in beauty all analogous subjects of British design. The transportation of such a heavy material, however, is not easy, as the Tay is not navigable above Perth.

There is also a beautiful yellow marble to be obtained, which is mottled with white; as likewise a coarse sort of white marble polluted with grey streaks.

The initials 'J.C.' carved by the stone mason between two bore holes in a block of untreated marble.

Up to eight men worked in the quarry and weekly output averaged four blocks, each weighing several tons and measuring from 3 feet to $8\frac{1}{2}$ feet, depending on demand. These huge blocks were then boxed and carted to Inver, near Dunkeld where there was a marble cutting mill and a polishing mill. By 1816 the marble was fetching a guinea a cubic foot in Edinburgh, with a William Reid being appointed agent. Unfortunately problems with quality soon arose with many of the blocks proving useless or too expensive to process. By 1830 cheaper foreign imports forced the price down to six shillings per cubic foot and it soon became uneconomic to continue.

Donald Macbeath

Clachglas (grey stone) 916 726 was also home to several generations of the Macbeath family, of whom Donald was the most famous son. He was born in 1831 and it is hardly surprising that Queen Victoria picked him out in 1861, as he was a man of great presence with an impressive war record who became Sergeant Major of the Atholl Highlanders and known in later years as 'the

Donald Macbeath, 'Father of the Regiment' and here in 1893, R.S.M. of the Atholl Highlanders.

father of the regiment'. In 1851 he enlisted in the Scots Fusilier Guards, was soon promoted to corporal and embarked with the regiment in 1854 for the Crimea. He took part in the battle of the Alma where his regiment, 'by its heroic conduct in circumstances of great difficulty, prevented what might have been a serious disaster.' After this he was promoted to sergeant and, as he was the best shot, was appointed the brigade sharpshooter. Because of this, he was constantly engaged in advance of his own trenches. He saw action at Balaclava and Inkerman, where he had no less than fourteen bullet holes in his clothes, but was himself unharmed. Writing to his father, who lived at Middlebridge in Glen Fender, on 29 January 1855, just before the Battle of Sebastopol, he wrote down his thoughts and feelings:

> The only thing I want now is to get home and see what is going on and see my friends once more. God was favourable to me and saved my life. Many a time I have been surrounded with russians but I paced them and got clean away without a scratch.

In another letter, dated 21 April 1855, he wrote:

> I was never better off in all my life. I am strong as a horse and as fat as a bullock. Our clothing is never off. We lay with our arms and accoutrements on and sometimes turn out between 2 & 3 in the morning for fear of an attack. There is twelve months now since I had my clothes off in the time.

On 6 September 1855 Donald rescued a sentry, Private Thomas Sankey, who had been badly wounded in advance of a covering party. Donald found himself in the Russian trenches and, under appalling conditions, carried the sentry to safety on his back. The citation for a gallantry medal was drawn up by Major Gerald Goodlake, Coldstream Guards as follows:

> **Date of act of Bravery 6th Sept. 1855**
> For having when in the right advanced sap in front of the Redan, volunteered to go out and look for the body of Captain Buckley, Sco. Fus. Guards who was supposed to be wounded – after seeing him safely carried by Sergeant Craig and a drummer – he went in search of Thomas Sankey who was dangerously wounded and carried him into the advanced sap – on his back under tremendous fire of grape and small arms.

Donald Macbeath was awarded the medal of Distinguished Conduct in the Field, although there were many who believed he merited the Victoria Cross for his incredible bravery.

Pol Te (woman's pool) 924 735 is in a bend of the river below Forest Lodge. On the east bank, in a settlement called Dail na Gaollsaich lived a man who was in the habit of stealing cattle from the tenants in Glen Fender. This upset his wife, who would release the stolen beasts from the pen where they were held. At length he became so cruel and vicious towards her that she could stand it no more and flung herself into the pool where she drowned.

Forest Lodge

Forest Lodge in 1810 before it was enlarged over a hundred years ago. (Sketch by Lady Emily Murray whose self-portrait appears in the bottom left-hand corner)

Forest Lodge 933 741, is eight miles up the glen from the castle and at the end of the track for motor car access. It is the only shooting lodge in the glen and was built in 1789. William Scrope described it in 1838:

> It is constructed without affectation of ornament and consists of two tenements united by a stone screen surmounted by stags' horns and in which there is an archway for carriages to pass.

A shooting party leaving Forest Lodge at the turn of the century.

One of these rooms, with a kitchen, was for the servants, while the other was for the laird and his guests, which meant that all food had to be carried across the open space. Apparently, once when the Duke of Buccleuch was renting the lodge, a haunch of venison was blown off its dish on a very windy night as it was being transported across. It was then 'dusted down' and presented as though nothing had happened!

Glen Tilt was renowned for its stalking and many of the finest stags have been shot in its steep confines. As many as eight hillmen could be employed in a shoot: the stalker with his telescope and knowledge of where to find the deer; men to carry rifles, several ponymen for taking the deer down and others to control dogs and gralloch the deer. There is little doubt that deer stalking had a vital part to play in employment in the glen up to the early part of this century.

Deer Driving

Towards the end of the last century, an American millionaire, Walter Winans rented the shooting rights in Glen Tilt. This man engendered the greatest derision and jealousy amongst Victorian sportsmen because his actions and methods were so contrary to their ideals of sportsmanship. Not only was he a fanatical deer stalker, but he had a passion for deer driving on a gigantic scale. He was a brilliant shot, known to have killed stags running at a gallop from a distance of over 200

The old Dail an Eas bridge beyond Forest Lodge fell down over twenty years ago. (Sketch by Lady Emily Murray)

Seventeen stags – the result of a deer drive in Glen Tilt by Walter Winans, an American millionaire.

yards, whereas for most, it was a challenge to shoot a stationary stag at a hundred yards. His drives were planned with all the thoroughness of a military operation and it was nothing for the tally to be over twenty stags in a day, aided by up to forty men and a great many ponies.

His own thoughts on stalking were written thus in 1913:

> Stalking as it used to be has entirely died out. We used to try to get within 60 yards, or even less of a stag; if he was 120 yards off, it was a very long shot, and 200 yards was out of range, practically. We used to, in consequence, have to stalk very well to get within range. Now with .275 rifles and telescopic sights, 200 yards is a very easy, sure shot and 300 yards no more difficult than 120 yards used to be. Stalking is therefore rendered very easy. . . As to running shots, I find I get nearly the double the number of beasts I should if I confined myself only to shooting an animal standing still, without counting the satisfaction of making a good running shot and turning the stag over like a rabbit. . . One should shoot running shots in preference, just as one does not shoot at sitting birds with shotguns since the old wheel-lock days.

Ruidh Allt a'Chrochaidh (shieling of the hanging burn) 958 765 is aptly named, as the stream drops here in a beautiful waterfall. In 1687 the shieling tenants paid no cash rent but a stone of cheese, a quart of butter and a sheep instead. Queen Victoria came here in 1844 on an excursion to watch Albert shooting and the party crouched in a low stone-walled bothy from where they had a spectacular view of the Beinn a' Ghlo corries where the hunters were. Beinn a' Ghlo is made up of a range of mountains and four of them: Carn nan Gabhar, the highest at nearly 3,700 feet (1,120m), Carn Liath, Braigh Coire Chruinn-bhalgain and Airgiod Bheinn are all over 3,000 feet (950m). There are twenty eight corries in the range and according to William Scrope:

> These corries, though contiguous, are separated from each other by such high ridges that a person standing in one of them could not hear a shot fired in the next.

Ruidh Allt a'Chrochaidh with the waterfall. Queen Victoria's 'hide' is in the foreground.

The Beinn a'Ghlo mountains, haunt of the Witch.

The Witch of Beinn a'Ghlo.

Witch of Beinn a' Ghlo

The Beinn a' Ghlo mountains were infamous for their witch who lurked among these immense corries. She was represented by William Scrope as:

> . . . of a very mischievous and malevolent disposition, driving cattle into morasses, where they perish, and riding the forest horses by night till covered with mire and sweat, they drop down from fatigue and exhaustion. She has the power of taking the shape of an eagle, raven, hind or any other animal that may suit her purpose. She destroys bridges. . .

This formidable creature was even more dramatically portrayed in a lengthy poem of fifty one verses by M G Lewis and here are four of them:

She heard him on her mount of stone,
Where on snakes alive she was feeding alone;
And straight her limbs she anointed all
With basilisk's blood and viper's gall.

But seeing, before away she sped
That her snakes half-eaten, were not yet dead,
She crush'd their heads with fiendish spite,
but had not the mercy to kill them quite.

Oh! then she mounted the back of the blast,
And sail'd o'er woods and waters fast;
She stopped on a rock awhile to rest,
And she throttled the young in an eagle's nest.

• • •

She stops for a moment to curse the grain,
Then away on the wind she hurries amain;
Now she flies high - now she flies low -
And lights on the summit of huge Ben-y-Gloe.

In *Historic Scenes in Perthshire* Dr. Marshall wrote that:

> In the latter part of the sixteenth century and the first part of the seventeenth, Athole was greatly infested with witches. . .

This was the peak time for witchcraft and witches were numerous in Atholl, regularly holding gatherings on a hill near Blair Atholl. There is an account that 'Margaret, Countess of Atholl was alleged to have been guilty of witchcraft in 1562', while Calderwood's History has a story of the witches of Atholl sending a present to Mary Queen of Scots in 1570:

> . . . About this time a present was sent, as was supposed from the witches of Atholl to the Scottish Queen; a prettie hart horne, not exceeding in quantitie the palm of a man's hand, covered with gold and artificiallie wrought. In the head of it were curiouslie engraven the armes of Scotland; in the nether part of it a throne, and a gentlewoman sitting in the same, in a robe royall, with a crown upon her head. Under her feet was a rose environed with a thistle. Under that were two lyons, the one bigger, the other lesser. The bigger lyon held his paw upon the face of the other, as his lord and commander. Beneath all were written these words - 'Fall what may fall, the lyon shall be the lord of all.'

The symbolism would imply that Mary was to triumph and be Queen of Scotland and England but in this case their prophecy was very wide of the mark!

A great convention was held in Atholl in 1597, supposedly attended by 2,300 witches. Shortly afterwards, Margaret Aitken was accused of being one of them, was tortured and confessed her guilt. To save herself she turned informer and disclosed the names of a great many local witches. Many of them were tried by the 'water ordeal' in which their thumbs and big toes were tied together and they were then flung into a loch or deep pool. If they sank and drowned they were innocent! If, however they floated they were deemed guilty and burned at the stake. It seems that justice in those times had a warped way of showing itself.

Vicious Assault

Dail Fheannach (shaggy haugh) 958 762 lies across the river from Allt a' Chrochaidh and was a farm of some twenty acres. John MacIntosh alias Odhar, lived here in the first half of the eighteenth century and was appointed forester in 1716:

> . . . he is obliged to kill 10 deer yearly and is to have half a crown for each hart and 20 pence for each hynd. . .

MacIntosh was viciously assaulted in 1732 by John Forbes from Ballentoul and the court records indicated:

> ... that his head was brock by the said John Forbes (without any cause given) to the effusion of his blood...

This incident took place in Wester Craggan and a witness, William Wallace from Old Bridge of Tilt said:

> ... he saw John Forbes take up a small ocken stick and struck John McIntosh upon the shoulder or his neck and at the same instance he saw John McIntosh draw a dirk and struck at the said John Forbes which he avoided by stepping aside and they struck at one another severall times and he saw John Forbes wounded in the head and shoulder with the dirk...

As he defended himself against Forbes, MacIntosh fell to the ground 'and his bonett and wig got off' and he was struck even more vigorously 'upon head, back and shoulders'. John Forbes's father, Mungo, who was building his kailyard dyke nearby entered the fray:

> ... fearing his son might be in hazard from the dirk, keaped down John Odhar and endeavoured to wrest the dirk out of Odhar's hands by which he gott himself a little blood in one of his fingers...

While Mungo Forbes held John MacIntosh on the ground, his son:

> ... offered him no manner of violence... and that upon the fray came several men out of the Smiddie and ale house and raised John Odhar and the dirk he had was given to a stranger minister that happened to be among them.

Mungo Forbes then 'beatt his sone with a horse whip (he had it in his hand he being going to a market) for the Ryot his sone had committed...'

The baillie of the court fined John Forbes £50 Scots and ordered him to pay John MacIntosh 'what charges he rely expends in cureing his hurt.'

A shieling close by, **Ruidh Allt Mheann** (shieling of the stream of the kids) 973 779 sits on such a steep part of the glen that level areas for the foundations of the bothies had to be dug out of the hillside. The location probably gives rise to its name as the slope was too steep for sheep to graze and more suited to goats.

Goats' milk was much prized in the Highlands and was considered the best for restoring strength to the weak, hence the Gaelic proverb:

> It is the milk of the goat, foaming and warm,
> that gives strength to the men that were.

According to another Highland proverb, goats' milk should also have found favour with young ladies, if they followed this advice:

> Rub thy face with violets and goats' milk and there is not a King's son in the world but will be after thee.

Next to that of deer, the tallow of the goat was thought to be the most efficacious for rubbing on stiff joints.

Near this shieling there is supposed to be a stone with the imprints of a man's and a dog's footprints, both pointing towards the river. While some regarded this as having supernatural undertones, others were of the opinion that they were merely the work of nature.

Within half a mile up-river, An Lochain flows into the Tilt at **Dail a' Chruineachd** (haugh of the grain) 980 783, a piece of flat ground opposite the ford mentioned as the farthest point in Lude's old boundary. Here are the ruins of a building, alleged to have been an inn, but there is no documentary evidence to support this. It was built over a three-week period in 1792 and thatched with heather. Queen Victoria stopped here for lunch on 9 October 1861 and described what she saw:

> ... looking up a glen towards Loch Loch, on a high bank overhanging the Tilt, looking back the view was very fine.

Two famous royal events took place in Glen Loch in the sixteenth century and they are covered in the next chapter.

Falls of Tarf

It is a mile further to the **Falls of Tarf** 982 796. Fording the river here was often dangerous and sometimes it was impassable. The glen folk, returning from Braemar with meal, were sometimes known to have lost part of it when attempting to cross the Tarf in spate. The old way to Fealar Lodge went over the hill from here and when it was burgled in 1822, eighteen bottles of claret were drunk and porter, hams and other things were removed by the thieves who lost a horse while attempting to ford the fast-flowing river. A single arch stone bridge was built over the Tarf in 1770, the work being undertaken by a mason, John Stewart, at a cost of £29.4s.0d. It was taken down by the estate in 1819 to try to deter foot traffic through the glen.

Queen Victoria and her party forded the Tarf on her way back to Balmoral in 1861 and her diary records the crossing:

> . . . A very few minutes brought us to the celebrated ford of the Tarff (Pol Tarff it is called) which is very deep, and after heavy rain, almost impassable . . . Sandy McAra, the guide, and the two pipers went first, playing all the time. To all appearances the ford of the Tarff was not deeper than the other fords, but once in it the men were above their knees - and suddenly in the middle, where the current, from the fine, high, full falls, is very strong, it was nearly up to the men's waists.

It was on 25 August 1879 that two young English students tried to cross the river, swollen by flood. One of them, after a terrible struggle, reached the other side, but the other, Francis John Bedford, a lad of eighteen, was swept away in the current, his body being found later, miles downstream. The two lads had taken off their clothes, tied them in bundles on their heads, so it was a naked youth, half-dead with cold, who later wandered into Forest Lodge and raised the alarm with James Macdonald, the stalker there. Seven years later the Bedford Bridge was built and named in memory of the young man who lost his life.

Glen Tarf

The Tarf (see map on page 48), the largest feeder river of the Tilt is more than ten miles long and its catchment area is in the mountains that form the Inverness-shire / Aberdeenshire boundary with Perthshire. The Falls of Tarf are particularly steep and treacherous and the story goes that some of

Queen Victoria and Prince Albert fording the Tarf in 1861. The cavalcade is guided by Charles Stewart, followed by two pipers, Aeneas Rose and Jock Macpherson. The 6th Duke of Atholl is leading the Queen's pony, with John Brown on her right and Sandy McAra to her left. Prince Albert rides behind the Queen with Princess Alice, whose pony is led by Donald Macbeath, beside him. Prince Louis of Hesse comes next with James Morgan, while General Grey is in the foreground, with Peter Robertson riding pillion. Next, Jock McAra leads Lady Churchill's pony, with John Grant and J. Smith behind, followed by five more of the Atholl hillmen.

the Fergusson clan were returning home this way, led by their chief, after a successful foray to the north. They had carried off some cattle and a fine black bull, which had been captured only after a great struggle, during which the Fergusson chief slew the bull's owner and his five sons. At the falls, the bull became restless and jumped down on to a rocky ledge overhanging a deep pool. 'Seamus Mor', or Big James, the chief's son leapt after it and tried to save it, but a big splash soon indicated that the bull had gone over the edge. When the chief saw his son appearing back above the ledge, he said scathingly: 'The soft grip of a baby; if you had been your father's son, you would have kept your grip.' At this, Seamus meekly replied, 'I have all I had', and tossed one of the bull's horns at his father's feet. Apparently he had caught hold of the bull by one of its horns at the moment it sprang off the ledge, and held it until the horn broke! Luckily the water was deep at this point and the bull was safely recovered. The chief's only comment was: 'The Clan Fergusson have not disintegrated yet.'

Craig an t-Suidh (stone of the hero) is a precipitous hill near the Falls of Tarf and three local men were passing this way one winter's day when the ground was frozen and icy. One of the men, Alex McGrigor, slipped and fell to his death. His two companions recovered his body and carried it to a shepherd's hut. One of them volunteered to go to Fealar for assistance, knowing there was a keeper called Cameron living there. No sooner had he departed than the hut was bombarded with stones and turfs. When the man who had stayed behind with the body went outside to investigate, the bombardment ceased - but restarted even more violently as soon as he went back inside, and eventually the man could stand it no longer and fled for his life. No satisfactory explanation was ever forthcoming to explain his eerie ordeal.

Feith Uaine Bothy

The **Feith Uaine bothy** (green streamlet) 927 789, now called the Tarf Bothy, is located five miles up Glen Tarf and was built at the end of the eighteenth century. When the factor visited it in 1799 he reported that it was in urgent need of repair as part of a side wall had fallen in and the roof was likely to collapse. A slated stone and lime house

The Feith Uaine bothy in Glen Tarf which was a favourite haunt of the 7th Duke of Atholl.

was built in 1806 but was burned down twenty years later as a deterrent to poachers who were using it as a shelter. It remained a ruin until the 1870s when the 7th Duke had it rebuilt, with wood-lined walls and a slated roof. In 1881 the hillmen's room was turned into an apartment for Louisa, the 7th Duchess and the old stables were converted into accommodation for the hillmen. In December 1883, a poor, deranged soul called Robertson, escaped from Murthly Asylum and went on the run. He broke into the bothy and spent several days there before being captured and taken back.

This was the most remote of the shooting lodges on the Atholl Estate and it soon became the favourite haunt of the 7th Duke who preferred its peace and solitude to the bustle and hilarity of Forest Lodge. Between 1872 and 1906 the Duke spent a total of 124 nights at Feith Uaine. His feelings are eloquently expressed in a letter to his sister-in-law, Lady Muir Mackenzie:

> Feith Uaine Bothy 9 miles beyond Forest Lodge and 1750 feet elevation.
> 2 Oct. 1906
> . . . I am so happy here, but it is terribly sad to me for I feel it is for the last time - I love this place. I made it & this night is the 13th that I have slept here . . . Why I say "for the last time" is because times are so bad that I fear Forest Lodge must be let now. . .

The march with Aberdeenshire is only three miles distant from there and runs across **An Sgarsoch** (the scree-covered slope) 933 836, a mountain of over 3,200 feet (985m). There is a tradition that a cattle and horse fair was held on the summit and

General view of the Feith Uaine bothy, drawn by the 7th Duke of Atholl, with the caption: 'His Grace roughing it in the Feith Uaine Bothy Aug. 1875'. The Duke is in bed and the Duchess is preparing breakfast.

traces of a rude causewayed road were found in the last century. The three counties of Perthshire, Aberdeenshire and Invernessshire meet three miles to the west at **Carn an Fhidleir** (fiddler's cairn) 904 842, which stands conspicuously on a ridge which is over 3,000 feet (925m) high.

An Sgarsoch mountain, framed by the ruin of the Rowan Tree bothy, which was occupied at the turn of the century by Robert 'Crom' Stewart, a hillman.

Half a mile beyond the Falls of Tarf and high up on the west side is **Ruigh Leth-chois** (shieling of one foot) 985 799 and this is the traditional place where Walter Comyn's horse was found, foaming at the mouth and riderless, save for a leg hanging from the stirrup. (See page 103 for the first part of the story) . Before this area developed as a place of summer pasture, it was renowned as the place where the hinds calved and as many as a thousand could be seen there at any one time.

At the confluence of two rivers, Allt Feith Lair and Allt Garbh Buidhe, which marks the start of the River Tilt, a ford points the way across to an old track climbing steeply on the other side, which is the old route to **Fealar** (stream of the mare) 009 800, two miles distant. Fealar stands 1,800 feet (550m) above sea level and had extensive grazing pastures. In 1752 there were nearly 750 animals grazing there and despite this number, the grass was described as being 'extremely good'. As many as 400 oxen were fattened there at any one time. Unlike the other local grazing areas, Fealar was leased to people outwith the area and nine various owners pastured their cattle here in 1758. Grazing rentals that year amounted to £60.10s.0d, offset by costs of £13.14s.4d, made up as follows:

	£	s	d
5 herds' wages	5	10	0
$9\frac{1}{2}$ bolls of meal	6	4	4
Advertising in the Lowlands	1	10	0
Payment, whisky etc to encourage herds		5	0
Postage etc. to advise owners when to collect cattle		5	0
	£13	14	4

Nota: 2 bottles of whisky cost 3 shillings.

Nowadays Fealar is used as a shooting lodge, with a resident keeper.

A Remarkable Wager

The lodge was built at the start of the nineteenth century, with Lord Kennedy and a Mr Skene, being the first tenants. The story of a remarkable wager is associated with Fealar. One of the Farquharsons of Invercauld wagered 2,000 guineas that Lord Kennedy could not, within 24 hours, from midnight to midnight, shoot forty brace of grouse then ride to Dunottar, near Stonehaven and back, a distance of 140 miles, in the time. Mr Turner was appointed umpire for Mr Farquharson and Captain Barclay for Lord Kennedy, with Mr Cumming acting as referee.

Fealar Lodge, the starting point for Lord Kennedy's remarkable wager and a haunt of poachers and the supernatural.

Lord Kennedy started for the hill at 4 a.m. on 12 August 1822, and though it had been a wet and windy night and the grouse were wild, he shot his first bird at 4.15 and by 9 am had collected his forty brace. Then it was back to the lodge for a quick change of clothes, a bite of breakfast and he set off for Dunottar on horseback at 9.30, arriving there at 2 p.m. Here he rested for an hour and was back in Fealar just before 8 pm. His time was just short of sixteen hours, so he easily won the wager. Not content with this, he then rode to Braemar, adding another fourteen miles to his tally, arriving there at 10 pm.

Strange Happenings

There have been many strange happenings in and around Fealar for which no logical explanations have ever been given. It not only afforded a night's lodgings for weary foot travellers but also acted as a base for more shady characters such as poachers. Two such came there after a day's poaching in Braemar, breaking into the lodge through a window as the door was locked. After kindling a fire, one of them went to collect some water and as he was climbing back in through the window, something unseen grabbed hold of his leg and held it in such a vice-like grip that he was at length only able to free himself with the greatest difficulty, his leg for ever afterwards bearing a mark. No doubt the two were happy enough to spend the rest of the night indoors!

Another incident took place to the north of Fealar after the 1745 uprising, when troops were stationed right across the Highlands. Twelve soldiers were quartered in Braemar Castle under the command of a Sergeant Davies who went off on a regular basis to collect their pay. On his return from one of these trips he was ambushed and shot dead by two men from Braemar who buried him on the moor and made off with the money. Some time later, a local shepherd had a vivid dream in which the sergeant's ghost told him his bones were lying in a moss five miles away and pleaded with the shepherd to have them interred properly in a churchyard after which he would trouble the shepherd no more. The bones were found in the very place described in the dream and a short time afterwards the two men were arrested as the suspected murderers. As no witness could be brought to testify except the shepherd who had had the dream, and his story was deemed unreliable, the men walked free at their trial. In after years however, one of them confessed his guilt on his deathbed.

About this time also, two Atholl men, James Robertson and Donald McEwan, who had fought at, and survived the Battle of Culloden, fled for safety up Glen Tilt to seek refuge on **Meall na Caillich Buidhe** (hill of the yellow woman) 999 809, a 2,000 feet (615m) high mountain, west of Allt Garbh Buidhe. Here they lurked for several days, but a woman from Strathardle found out they were there and informed the soldiers stationed in Kirkmichael of their whereabouts and they came and surrounded the place whilst the two men slept. Despite being naked and without weapons, the men put up a strong resistance and eventually the sergeant shot Robertson, for fear of the twelve being overcome. In the confusion, McEwan fled, naked, with shots all around him, and escaped to Braemar where he was concealed by friends. When Robertson's family heard what had befallen him, they brought his body down on a horse and buried him in Struan churchyard.

Poaching

There are a great many stories about hunting and poaching in the remote countryside around Fealar and the most famous poacher of them all was a man called Lonavey, who had only one hand, cut off years before, as a punishment for shooting in the Forest of Atholl. Despite this handicap he won many prizes for his skill in shooting. Eventually he was caught again and tried for poaching and confined to Perth prison, where, just before he died, he confided to a fellow inmate, the whereabouts of his concealed gun. Just before his arrest he had hidden his gun and dirk in a cave on **Carn nan Righ** (the king's cairn) a 3,000 feet (925m) mountain, traditionally named after King Malcolm who often hunted there. To preserve his gun, Lonavey had smeared it with deer tallow and placed it in such a way, that on one day a year, the sun's rays would shine on it. Many years later, another famous poacher, John Farquharson, shot a stag on Carn nan Righ and was on the point of gralloching it, when three keepers came into view. He quickly concealed himself in a cave he luckily stumbled on, and as his eyes became accustomed to the gloom, he discovered the remains of the Lonavey gun.

It is only two miles from the Falls of Tarf to the county march between Perthshire and Aberdeenshire and most of this part of the route is little more than a mere footpath winding along the hillside, in many places above a steep gorge. The watershed is marked by **Dubh Alltan** (little black stream) 000 825 which flows within a few yards of the march. Many years ago, a band of men from Mar, armed with picks and shovels came here and attempted to dig a trench through the level ground, to divert this stream so that it would flow into the Dee rather than the Tilt. An opposing band of men from Atholl were sent in time to stop them, so the course of Dubh Alltan remained unchanged.

Loch Tilt 993 827 lies in a hollow in the hills above the watershed and when Thomas Pennant stopped beside it for lunch in 1769, he wrote:

> . . . Dined on the side of Loch Tilt, a small piece of water, swarming with Trouts.

And it still is!

As the last vale to be exalted,
As the last hill to be made low,
Out of thy loving kindness Lord,
Leave us Glen Tilt and Beinn a' Ghlo.

Aerial view of Loch Tilt on the watershed – 'swarming with Trouts'.

Beautiful Loch Loch at the centre of the Seven Shielings, seen from the south. Mary Queen of Scots was stationed on a knoll at the south end to observe the royal hunt.

At the place where the two sides of Loch Loch almost meet, it is possible to wade across.

CHAPTER FOUR

GLEN LOCH

Glen Loch (see map on page 48) is less than three miles from Glen Tilt to its head at Loch Loch and can aptly be described as a royal glen because of two major events which took place in it, within forty years of each other in the sixteenth century.

The area of level ground on the east side of the confluence of the **Lochain Burn** 980 786 and the Tilt was the site of a royal feast in 1529, when King James V of Scotland, accompanied by his mother, Queen Margaret and the Pope's ambassador, stayed there for three days to take part in lavish entertainment, including a royal hunt. John, the 3rd Earl of Atholl, known for his extravagant hospitality, had assembled hundreds of his followers to form an immense circle and channel the deer, over a period of days, towards the site of the hunt.

The Earl was anxious to demonstrate his power and wealth by entertaining his guests in as lavish a manner as they would receive in Edinburgh. Walter Scott, in his *Tales of a Grandfather*, gives us a detailed account of the arrangements:

> On one occasion, when the King had an ambassador of the Pope along with him, with various foreigners of distinction, they were splendidly entertained by the Earl of Athole in a huge and singular rustic palace. It was built of timber, in the midst of a quiet meadow, and surrounded by moats or fosses, full of the most delicate fish. It was enclosed and defended by towers, as if it had been a regular castle, and had within it many apartments, which were decked with flowers and branches, so that in treading them one seemed to be in a garden. There were all kinds of game and other provisions in abundance, with many cooks to make them ready, and plenty of most costly spices and wines. The Italian Ambassador was greatly surprised to see, amongst rocks and wildernesses, which seemed to be the very extremity of the world, such good lodgings and so magnificent an entertainment. But what surprised him most of all was to see the Highlanders set fire to the wooden castle as soon as the hunting was over and the King in the act of departing. "Such is the constant practice of our Highlanders," said James to the Ambassador; "however well they may be lodged over the night, they always burn their lodging before they leave it." By this the King intimated the predatory and lawless habits displayed by these mountaineers.

It was said to have cost the Earl £1,000 a day for this display, and throughout the three-day stay, two hundred deer, a wolf, a fox and several wild cats were killed. It is hard to imagine a more costly, yet effective way of impressing these prestigious guests - perhaps in our times, of disposing of a Rolls Royce when the ashtray is full!

Vestiges of the palace were still visible two hundred years ago, but since then the ravages of

The confluence of the Tilt and the Lochain Burn. The level piece of ground to the left was the site of the elaborate wooden palace built to entertain James V in 1529.

time and weather have obliterated all traces of the festivities. The **Lochain bothy** 982 782 is located a few hundred yards upstream and was built over 120 years ago, but as it became an alleged haunt of poachers was later burned down.

Shieling Dispute

There is scarcely a path at all up the glen to Loch Loch and here, on the west side, is **Ruigh na Cuile** (shieling of the wind) 985 757, where the remains of over twenty shieling huts can still be seen, spread out along the hillside. This shieling was the subject of violence and litigation between Atholl and Robertson of Lude.

The problem arose because Atholl insisted that the shieling lay between two of his deer forests and that the people living there in common with their cattle, prevented the free passage of deer. The case came before the Court of Regality in Blair Castle, on 7 July 1679, when the Marquis of Atholl lost his case.

Under pretext of maintaining order in the area, he formed a local militia called the 'Watch', which invaded the shieling on 3 July 1680 and built a small bothy on it. This was promptly demolished by Lude and his tenants who 'did make civil interruption by casting down of certain divots [turfs] and timbers of the said bothie'. Some years later the 'Watch' secretly rebuilt the bothy, which was again removed by Lude.

The case came up again in the Regality Court on 7 July 1687, when Lude produced a number of witnesses to testify his right to the shieling: John Robertson of Easter Straloch, aged seventy, said he knew the shieling to be part of Lude for the past fifty years, with no interruption until the past few years. Donald Robertson from Calvine said that thirty four years earlier he stopped at the shieling and drank milk and that then it belonged to Lude. Robert Gray from Lyncondlich, aged eighty six, maintained it had always been part of Lude and that as a young man he had worked in the shieling when there were eleven other men also working there. It was not until 1716 that the matter was finally resolved and then very much in Atholl's favour.

Big Comyn

Loch Loch is a beautiful loch in the steep confines of the Beinn a' Ghlo mountains. About a mile and

The remains of Comyn's Cairn beside Loch Loch, where Big Comyn met his spectacular end.

Extract from a 1790 'Draught of the Barony and Lands of Lude...' which shows two lochs, leading to the origination of the name Loch Loch.

a half in length, it is somewhat in the shape of a fiddle and at one point the two sides almost meet, making it possible to wade across there. It gets its name because there appears to be two lochs and old maps certainly confirm this. **Comyn's Cairn** 987 755 is located on the east side of the loch, near its north end, and is a small, rather insignificant heap of stones, about six feet across and only eighteen inches high, yet its history far outweighs its appearance.

In the beginning of the fourteenth century, Atholl was split between the Comyns of Ruthven, Earls of Badenoch and the MacIntoshes of Tirinie, Thanes of Glen Tilt. The wife of Big Comyn had a voracious appetite and it was said that 'she devoured a choppin [quart] of beef marrow every day, besides a profusion of other dainties'. Knowing this, at Christmas time, the MacIntosh chief presented the lady with a prize bull and twelve cows, but instead of being grateful for his generosity, Comyn cast covetous eyes on the MacIntosh herd of cattle and the Tirinie pasture land. One night he and his men surrounded the MacIntosh castle at Tom-a-Mhuir, murdered the family and seized their possessions.

An old man called **Croit a'Bhoineide** (bonnet croft), so named because he gave the laird a new bonnet as his annual rent, getting the old one back, lived nearby. Next morning he went to the castle to pay his rent and was horror-struck at the butchery he found. In what he thought would be a vain hope of finding anyone still alive, he came across MacIntosh's baby son, Ewan, unharmed in a cradle. In the greatest secrecy the old man took the child to his mother's relatives, the Campbells of Achnabreck in Argyll. There the child was raised, unaware of who he really was and of the tragedy that had befallen his family. By the age of eighteen he was a renowned archer and when Croit a' Bhoineide saw him hit the bullseye every time, told him, 'The grey breast of the man who killed your father is much broader than that target' and went on to recount the terrible fate that his family had been subjected to. The young man gathered together a band of thirty well-armed men and set out for Atholl to gain revenge.

On arrival in Atholl, Ewan learned that Big Comyn was celebrating the marriage of one of his retainers in a nearby house. He split his men into two groups, posting one between the house and Blair Castle and proceeding with the other to attack the house. When the alarm was raised, Comyn attempted to return to the castle but finding the way blocked, fled up Glen Tilt, hotly pursued by Ewan. Comyn headed for Loch Loch and was running along the east side, with Ewan on the other bank, when he sat on a stone to rest. He was in the act of wiping perspiration from his brow, when Ewan shot him dead from across the loch, a distance of a quarter of a mile, pinning Comyn's hand to his forehead in the process. The spot is marked by the small cairn and this event ended the dominance of the Comyns in Atholl.

Seven Shielings

Loch Loch lies in the centre of an area called the Seven Shielings, now remote and deserted, but two hundred years ago there were hundreds of people working in the summer shielings. A first-hand description of a shieling in operation comes from Hugh Miller:

> The bothy is a rude, low-roofed erection of turf and stone with a door in the centre, of some five feet in height or so, but with no window. It has a slim pillar of smoke ascending from the roof. There is a turf fire at one end of the room and the other end was occupied by a bed of straw. The inmates of the shieling were employed in making butter and cheese for their master, when the pasture was at its best, and lived there for several months each year.

The lairds imposed strict regulations on the shieling season and tenants were obliged to adhere to these:

> 4 March 1710
> None shall stay at home from their shealing after the first of June with their cows or sheep - penalty 40/- Scots.
>
> 1 November 1723
> . . . be off to the shealings on or about June 1st and that none be either behind their neighbours in going or before them in coming from the shealings under penalty of a good wedder [sheep].

Stringent rules also applied to livestock grazed on

Occupants of shielings made butter and cheese in the summer.

the shielings and the pasturing of swine was curbed, with penalties for those found breaking the rules:

> 17 April 1628
> None to hold swyne without permission, penalty £5.
>
> 6 July 1666
> Nae tennant keip swyne – and especiallie any sort of swyne that shall be fund within the bounds of Glen Loch pasturing thier and in that case the said swyne belongs to the Laird.
>
> 28 November 1721
> Whoever having swine shall be oblidged to ring them in the nose or to give one yearly to Lude and to keep them, each person upon his own possession with full liberty to any person who shall see another swine not ringed (upon his possession) to kill these swine at his pleasure.
>
> 14 March 1734
> Damage caused by swyne – particularly thier dinging down of dikes and plantings and ditches besides the harm to cornland and grass – 12/- for each swine unringed – to be disposed of also at his [the laird's] pleasure.

The general unpopularity of the tenants keeping swine is shown not only by these regulations but also by the following incidents in the 1760s when Lude's tenants' swine in the Seven Shielings were being seized by Atholl foresters as the following reports show:

> Dunkeld 24 June 1762
> . . . saw one of the fforesters who told him that Ludes Tennants Swine had been in the Grounds of Seven Sheallings, upon which he (Harrison) drove the Swine out of the Bounds of the Forrest. The owners acknowledged that they were theirs and as such drove them back again, so that there can be no doubt of proveing whose property they are. This has been done oftener than once since the Season began of being in the Seven Sheallings with their cattle. What is more extraordinary the fforester also said that the Swine was drove back again by Lude's particular orders. . .

The affair rumbled on during the summer:

> Dunkeld 6 August 1762
> . . . the fforester went to the fforest on Monday morning last and seized and Ingathered from Lude's sheallings a parcell of swine consisting of 36 in number. They brought them to Blair that evening and housed them in a large Barn where grass and Water was laid before them. Lude was not at home but some of the Tennants and owners of the swine was at Blair Monday evening & saw them housed. They were told that the swine would be liberated on payment of a merk each, viz., the half merk in the Act for Winter Herding and half a merk for the dammage done all this Summer in the fforest. But they said they were not at Freedom to redeem them at any rate without orders from their Master. Tuesday they came again to Blair and told the same thing. . . An express was sent to Lude - 'who had positively discharged his tenants from relieving the Swine or to pay any consideration whatever nor take any further notice of them'.

The agitation of the factor was becoming apparent as it was costing the estate money to house and feed the beasts and possible compensation if they were to die. The letter continues:

> So that they still remain in the Barn. You will please without loss of time [say] what Step is next to be taken, Because so many of these Ravenous Animals confined soon Die or Destroy one another and there is no other way of keeping them together but in a House. 3 of the Swine belonged to one of My Lord Duke's tennants who redeemed them yesterday - the 33 belonging to Lude's people.

More stringent measures were resorted to over a week later:

> Dunkeld 15 August 1762
> . . . Mr Wood the Baron Baillie was writt to who came here on Wednesday 11th and made Intimation under form of Instrument which they did to Lude's servant . . . likewise to said owners of the swine to come to Blaïr Thursday 12th to receive the swine and pay the legall penalty. . .

The owners were cited to appear, with their pigs being valued at '£6 odds' apiece, with the additional money penalties for damage and fodder, but they were not redeemed and:

> . . . the swine were sold next day at £5 Sterling, as the most that could be made of them. . .

There is a little footnote to this affair:

> Atholl House 26 October 1762
> I am glad now to tell you that you will have no more trouble about Lude's affair, hostilitys having ended on both sides.

Not only were there disputes about the shieling livestock, but during the seventeenth, eighteenth and nineteenth centuries there were interminable disputes over land uses and rights. One of the root causes was that whereas Atholl had the superiority of tenure of the land, Lude initially owned the grazing rights. This meant that Atholl had the authority to order Lude's tenants off any area he wished to hunt in, which obviously provided fertile grounds for lengthy litigation.

In a charter of 1679, John, Marquis of Atholl was granted ownership to the land, but Lude was given the right to pasture, fowling, hunting and fishing. This agreement changed when Alexander Robertson of Carnoustie, Lude's brother, was captured for taking part in the 1715 Jacobite uprising and locked up in Blair Castle. Applications to free him were in vain, as the Duke insisted on the payment of a fine of £10,000 Scots, which Lude was unable to afford and in order to save his brother's life, agreed to rigorous terms and conditions concerning the Seven Shielings, which resulted in his having 'a bare servitude of pasturage' for three months in the year. He lost his right to hunting and his tenants were obliged to remove themselves at least eight days in advance of Atholl hunting across the land.

Hunting Rights

There were a number of occasions when Atholl said he planned to hunt across the Seven Shielings and then cancelled at the last moment, in order, apparently, to annoy Lude and his tenants. In September 1791, Lude received a letter from the Duke, detailing his plans for later in the month:

> . . . I wish to inform you that I propose hunting on the grounds of the Seven Shielings on Thursday 22nd of this month and I have to request that you will give orders for these grounds being cleared of yours and your tenants' sheep and cattle in confirming the terms of the decreet and under which conditions you have the servitude of grassing on my lands. I further wish that you would give instructions to your own shepherd and to your tennants who grass there in future to refrain from burning the heather on these bounds. . .

What Lude's feelings were on the receipt of such a letter, can best be left to the imagination.

In September 1801 a hunt did take place, with invitations to 'a grand hunt at Blair' being sent out to the Duke's friends and neighbours. A proclamation was even read out at St Bride's church door on the previous Sunday, telling tenants to report to the castle the day before the hunt. Several hundred turned up and were handed ropes, being told to spread out as far as possible, so that a line of several miles was formed, covering a huge area of land. Then a semi-circle was formed and they advanced towards the Seven Shielings, the idea being to force all the deer into the area of the hunt, where the Duke and his friends would be waiting. Whatever the cause, not a single deer was killed that day!

The names of the Seven Shielings were:

1. **Creagan Gorm** (little green rocky place) 976 677.
2. **Allt na H-Eachdra** (stream of the pen) 957 687.
3. **Ruidh na Cloiche** (shieling of the stone) 970 704.
4. **Ruidh na H-Eilrig** (shieling of the deer enclosure) 970 707.
5. **Ruidh Chuilean** (shieling of the whelp) 994 729.
6. **Ruidh Sron nan Dias** (shieling of the point of the blade) 994 729.
7. **Leacainn Diollaidh** (saddle slope) 987 732.

Ruidh na H-Eilrig is near the confluence of two rivers where a large expanse of green pasture is on a gently rising slope. Elrigs were often found

Ruidh na H-Eilrig below Carn nan Gabhar.

on rising ground in an open area, flanked by water. Here the King or chief, with his visiting hunters, would wait, all armed, while his men drove the deer from miles around into this manned enclosure which was barricaded on three sides. The hounds were then unleashed and as many deer as possible were slaughtered by bow and arrow or by the sword. A John Stewart from Blair Atholl was famed for cutting a deer clean in two with a single stroke of his broadsword.

Leacainn Diollaidh was famous for its saddle-shaped fertility stone, after which it is named. The tradition was that any woman who was apparently unable to conceive a child, made a pilgrimage to this shieling in Glen Loch where she sat on the Saddle Stone, and in due course of time, became pregnant. This custom evidently continued until the start of the nineteenth century.

Mary Queen of Scots

The most famous Atholl hunt of all took place in August 1564 when the second royal event occurred in Glen Loch. At that time, Mary Queen of Scots visited the Perthshire Highlands as the guest of the Earl of Atholl when she and her party attended a hunt at the south end of the loch. The Queen was stationed on a knoll, now called **Tom nan Ban Righ** (the Queens hillock) from where she observed the proceedings. An account of this hunt was given by a scholar called Professor Barclay, who was one of the Queen's party as a young man:

> The Earl of Athole, a prince of the royal blood, had, with much trouble and vast expense, a hunting match for the entertainment of our most illustrious and most gracious Queen. Our people call this a royal hunting. I was then a young man, and was present on this occasion. Two thousand Highlanders, or wild Scotch, as you call them here, were employed to drive to the hunting ground all the deer from the woods and hills of Athole, Badenoch, Mar, Murray and the counties about. As these Highlanders use a light dress, and are very swift of foot, they went up and down so nimbly that in less than two months' time they brought together 2000 red deer, besides roes and fallow deer. The Queen, the great men, and others, were in a glen when all the deer were brought before them. Believe me, the whole body of them moved forward in something like battle order. This sight still strikes me, and ever will, for they had a leader whom they followed close wherever he moved. This leader was a very fine stag, with a very high head. The sight delighted the Queen very much; but she soon had occasion to fear, upon the Earl's (who had been accustomed to such sights) addressing her thus:- 'Do you observe that stag who is foremost of the herd? There is danger from that stag; for if either fear or rage should force him from the ridge of that hill, let every one look to himself, for none of us will be out of the way of harm; for the rest will follow this one, and having thrown us under foot, they will open a passage to this hill behind us.' What happened a moment after confirmed this opinion, for the Queen ordered one of the best dogs to be let loose upon a wolf; this the dog pursues, the leading stag was frightened, and he flies by the same way he had come there, the rest rush after him, and break out where the thickest body of Highlanders was. They had nothing for it but to throw themselves flat upon the ground and allow the deer to pass over them. It was told the Queen that several of the Highlanders had been wounded, and that two or three had been killed outright, and the whole body had got off had not the Highlanders, by their superior skill in hunting, fallen upon a stratagem to cut off the rear from the main body. It was one of those that had been separated that the Queen's dog and those of the nobility made slaughter. There were killed that day 360 deer, with five wolves and some roes.

The practice of muir burning was carried out on the shielings in the spring of the year. On average two or three acres were burned at a time, although in a dry season this could increase to six or seven acres. It was always the longest heather that was burned, leaving behind roots and stumps to be used as fuel the following year. The idea behind this practice was not only to increase the pasture area, but also to improve the feeding value.

Lude, as we have seen, seldom lost an opportunity to thwart the Duke's hunting and he did so in a fairly spectacular fashion on one occasion, when over 4,000 acres of moorland were set alight, in an effort, it was said, to drive all the deer off his pasture and put an end, once and for all to the Duke's hunting sorties.

Atholl raised an Action for Muir Burning against Lude in 1809 at which witnesses testified, including James MacDonald who shieled at Craggangorm and said that he:

> . . . felt that the whole burnings over the whole of the seven shielings land was not less than 200 acres in some years. . . He remembered seeing 45 of Ludes tennants shieling on the seven shielings.

James McLaren who had a shieling in Ruidh na H-Eilrig testified that burning took place in Glen Loch:

> . . . to an extent of 15 acres. He had seen heather to the extent of 10 acres burnt in the other shealings. Had seen others burn small bits, to set turfs for thatching their shealing bothies.

John Robertson, from Bohespick, aged 37 years, said 'most of the heather was burnt at Ben Vurich'.

Ben Vuirich (mountain of the bellowing) 997 700 is the 2,962 foot (903m) mountain which dominates Glen Loch from the south. Its name is supposed to come from the roaring of wolves, reckoned to be the largest and most ferocious in the area. This is also mentioned in *Oran Nam Beann*, one of the most ancient poems known in Atholl:

I see Ben Ghlo of the pointed tops
Ben Bheag and Argiod Bheann
Ben Bhuirich of the great wolves
And the brook of the Bird's Nest by its side.

The misty outline of Ben Vuirich at the southern end of Loch Loch.

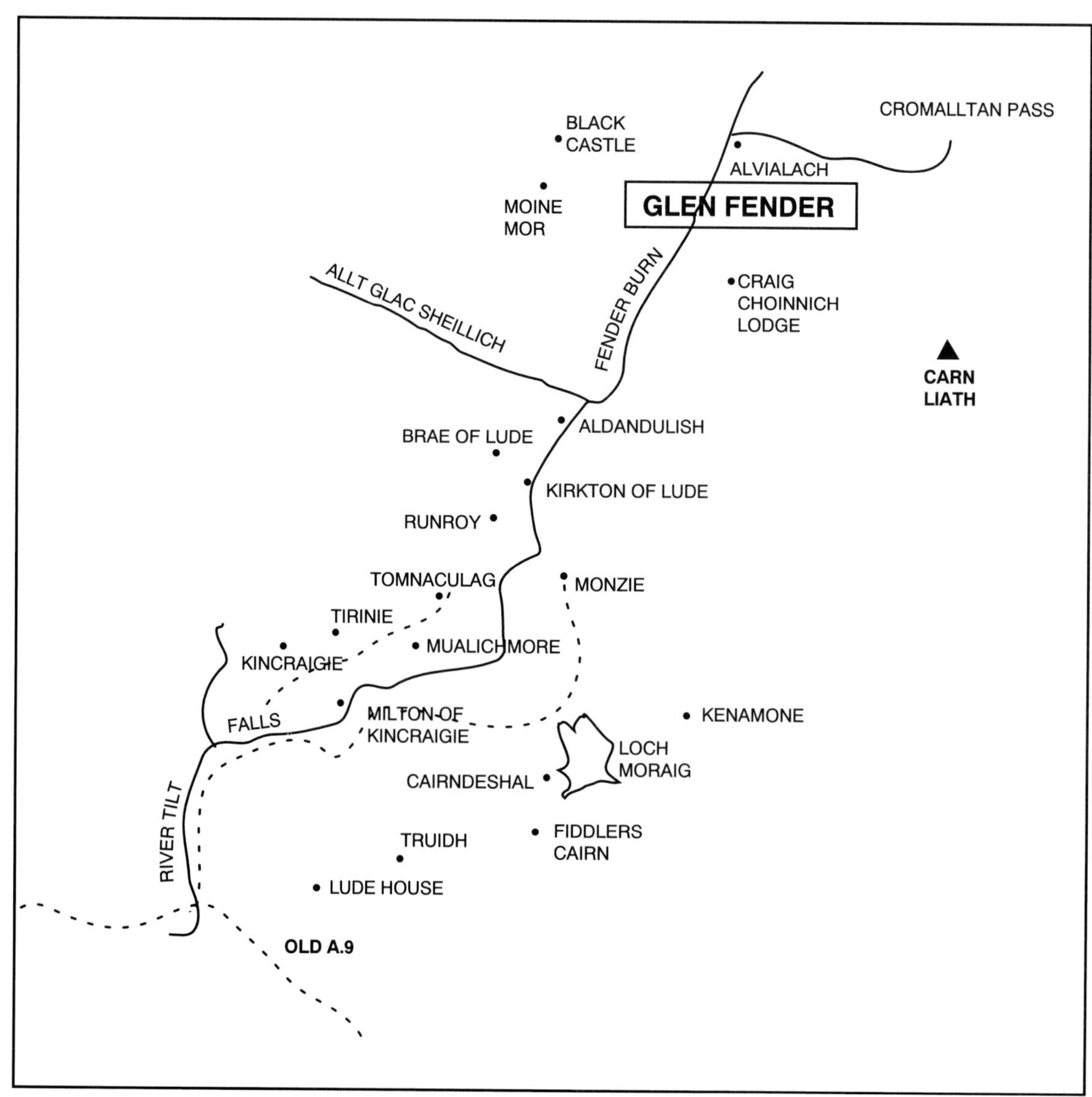
CROMALLTAN PASS
BLACK CASTLE
ALVIALACH
MOINE MOR
GLEN FENDER
ALLT GLAC SHEILLICH
FENDER BURN
CRAIG CHOINNICH LODGE
CARN LIATH
ALDANDULISH
BRAE OF LUDE
KIRKTON OF LUDE
RUNROY
TOMNACULAG
MONZIE
TIRINIE
MUALICHMORE
KINCRAIGIE
FALLS
MILTON OF KINCRAIGIE
KENAMONE
LOCH MORAIG
CAIRNDESHAL
RIVER TILT
TRUIDH
FIDDLERS CAIRN
LUDE HOUSE
OLD A.9

CHAPTER FIVE

GLEN FENDER

The Fender Burn rises in the southern slopes of Carn Liath and tumbles into the Tilt at the Falls of Fender, six miles below. Much of the north side belonged to Atholl, including the lands of Kincraigie and Tirinie which were held under feu. Donald Robertson, brother of Alexander Robertson of Lude, became the laird in 1615 and was instrumental in bringing out the men of Atholl to join Montrose when he raised the Royal Standard in July 1644 on the **Truidh** 893 662, a hill above Lude with commanding views of both Glen Garry and Glen Tilt, the main routes into Atholl. Over 800 men flocked to join the royalist cause. Angus Cameron, now living at Mains of Orchil, remembers ploughing the hillside in the 1940s and seeing the cairn which marked the spot where the standard was raised, but it is now enveloped by a field clearance heap.

'Bonnie' Dundee led his army up Glen Fender, behind Lude House in 1689, skirted past Loch Moraig and took up his position on the high ground above Urrard, thus gaining the advantage of height prior to the Battle of Killiecrankie:

> Short was the foregathering which King James's people made of it, up one side of the hill they charged, copiously poured the sweat from each brow, as they ascended the north side of the Pass.

A general view of Glen Fender looking towards Carn Liath.

Angus Cameron pointing out the remains of the cairn on the Truidh where the Marquis of Montrose raised the standard in 1644.

By 1727 Kincraigie had passed to Donald's grandson, also Donald, who by the 1750s was in 'straitened circumstances', particularly regarding his tenants to whom he owed thousands of pounds. The situation became so acute that in 1761 he sold off the estate, part of it to his son, Charles and the balance to Atholl. Towards the end of his life he had the satisfaction of clearing off all his debts, having vowed 'he would not taste liquor of any kind till his business was over'. Though infirm with gout and rheumatism he went to the church 'to make further declarations of his sales in public'.

Although geographically in Glen Tilt, for rental and economic reasons the settlement of **Kincraigie** (head of the crag) 884 675 was included with Glen Fender, as it still is today.

In 1764, Angus Robertson of the Mill of Kincraigie accused Alex Graham, a servant of Donald Stewart of Shierglas, of stealing from his shieling. Later this accusation was withdrawn and Angus's vindication of his character was read out in church:

I Angus Robertson, Tacksman of the Miln of Kincraigie hereby declare that I am now fully convinced that Alex Graham servant to Donald Stewart of Shierglas, did not steal any cheese or cream or anything else whatsoever, out of my shieling of RieNeill [Glen Tilt] and I am very sorry. . .

Milton of Kincraigie before modernisation in the last century and the home of William McAra who was hopelessly in debt in the 1820s.

Alex Seaton, a Kincraigie tenant, was so heavily in arrears with his rent, that in 1798 the Atholl factor was forced to act by issuing a 'Decreet of Removing with Poind and Arrest':

> Decreet of Removing. . . Alexander Seaton in Kincraigie. I command you that on sight hereof, ye pass and charge the said defender personally or at their dwelling places to flit remove themselves their wives, bairns, servant, families, subtenants, dependers, goods and gear forth and from the houses, mills, yards, grass and sheallings at and against the term of Whitsunday next Old Style on the 26th May new and from the arable and laboured lands at and against the separation of the ensuing crop from the ground and that under the pain of ejection as also each of the defenders to pay the complainer £20 Scots in name of damages and expences in case they find that within fifteen days next after the charge. . . that ye lawfully fence and arrest the said defenders goods gear and debts. . .

Rent Arrears

Problems of rent arrears became very acute in the 1820s and the case of William McAra, the Kincraigie tenant, illustrates the tactics used to delay and evade payment.

William McAra leased the mill at Kincraigie and a pendicle (small piece of land) nearby. In 1816 his arrears totalled £43.13.0 and as he paid no rent the following year, a further £55 was added to his debt which then totalled £98.13.0. He then paid £21.15.0 and promised 'most faithfully' to pay off the balance within fourteen days.

1816	Arrears	£43 13 0
	1 year's rent due	55 0 0
		98 13 0
	Less payment	21 15 0
1817	Outstanding arrears	£76 18 0

No payment was made as the rent collector found it impossible to get hold of McAra for several months and by this time the next half year's rent of £27.10.0 was due. When he eventually caught up with McAra, all he could persuade him to pay was £25.10.0, leaving his debt virtually unchanged:

	Arrears	£76 18 0
	Half year's rent due	27 10 0
		104 8 0
	Less payment	25 10 0
1818	Outstanding arrears	£78 18 0

Another half year's rent became due and in May 1819 McAra made a payment of £61.15.0, thus considerably reducing his debt:

	Arrears	£78 18 0
	Half year's rent due	27 10 0
		106 8 0
	Less payment	61 15 0
1819	Outstanding arrears	£44 13 0

When McAra was pressed for full payment, the collector observed that:

> . . . according to his usual custom, he told me a great many lies and pitiful stories about his misfortunes that I ascertained never to have happened to him and I told him that unless he gave me his Bill for the arrears, proceedings would be adopted against him. He knew that the Bill would enable me to attack his person and make innumerable difficulties.

McAra duly signed the Bill confirming his rent arrears and solemnly promised to pay it when his next half year payment was due in August 1819. The collector was not impressed, reporting that 'the man was too slippery to be trusted in the least', and persuaded him to pay £19.0.0, thus reducing his arrears:

	Arrears	£44 13 0
	Less payment	19 0 0
1819	Outstanding arrears	£25 13 0

The collector's report continued:

> From some particulars of the man's conduct I was convinced he contemplated a moonlight flitting. I therefore sequestrated his stock and crop and procured a horning [court direction forcing a debtor to pay] and had him arrested and brought only to Dunkeld without sending him to Perth as I thought the apprehension of being sent further might persuade him at least

> to play no tricks, at least if not to pay up his arrears. He made the most solemn promise to pay up all he was owing, if he was set at liberty and he was accordingly released.

His next half year's rent was due at Martinmas (November) and of this he could only manage a payment of £20.0.0. The following May when the next rent payment came due he paid off a further £20.0.0. reducing his debt to just over £40.0.0:

	Arrears	£25 13 0
	Half year's rent due	27 10 0
		53 3 0
	Less payment	20 0 0
		33 3 0
	Half year's rent due	27 10 0
		60 13 0
	Less payment	20 0 0
1820	Outstanding arrears	£40 13 0

The following year his rent was increased to £60 and in order to keep his debt at £40 he made a payment of £60:

	Arrears	£40 13 0
	Year's rent due	60 0 0
		100 13 0
	Less payment	60 0 0
1821	Outstanding arrears	£40 13 0

McAra then tried to have the arrears of £40 wiped off, by claiming that the mill machinery was in need of repair and 'was dangerous to work at present'. The collector continued:

> I have a letter from McAra with a clumsy attempt to try to set aside his last Bargain for the Pendicle, the rent of which he states to be included in what he is charged for the Mill - but as the amount of this new rent has never been mentioned to him by any person from the time I saw him in Spring 1820 till I received his letter, it appears that he and his adviser who is supposed to be Williamson's confidential clerk, have merely overreached themselves in this attempt to cheat.
>
> The repair of the Mill I have all along told him would be taken into consideration as soon as his Rent should be cleared. . .

Within a year the mill ceased to operate and the lease of the land passed to Alex Gow.

The lands of Lude were formed into a barony by royal charter in 1448, occupying the ground east of the River Tilt and mostly south of the Fender Burn.

The original Lude House was situated in the upper part of Glen Fender, somewhere near the church at Kirkton of Lude, but it was razed to the ground by Cromwellian troops in the 1650s and in spite of extensive fieldwork, no trace of it can be seen today. After this, the Robertsons moved down the glen and built a new home where the present Lude House now stands.

Lude Harps

The Robertsons in north Perthshire were famed both for their own skill in playing the harp and in having talented harpers in their employ. There are two famous harps in existence: the Lamont Harp and the Lude Harp. The latter of these, sometimes called the Queen Mary Harp was by tradition given in 1564 by Mary Queen of Scots during her Atholl hunting visit (see page 82), to Beatrix Gardyn, wife of John Robertson of Lude, because of her own skill in playing. Evidence of the Lude Robertsons themselves playing the harp comes from a story told by the Rev. Donald MacIntosh, about 'Laird John', a famous performer, who died in 1731:

> One night my father said to Lude that he would be happy to hear him play upon the harp, which at that time began to give place to the violin. After supper Lude and he retired to another room, in which there were a couple of harps, one of which belonged to Queen Mary. "James", says Lude, "here are two harps, the largest one is the loudest, but the small one is the sweetest; which do you wish to hear played?" James answered: "The small one", which Lude took up and played upon until daylight.

The last recorded public performance of the Lude harp took place on 2 September 1745 at a ball given in Lude House in honour of Charles Edward Stuart, then on his triumphant march to Edinburgh and the south. According to Jacobite Memoirs, 'the Prince was very cheerful, and took his share in several dances such as minuets and Highland reels.'

In the first part of the nineteenth century the harp passed out of the hands of the Robertsons to the Stewarts of Dalguise, eventually passing into the care of the National Museum in Edinburgh, where it still is today.

The Hon. Mrs Robertson (Lady Lude) figured conspicuously in Atholl in the Rising of 1745, hosting a ball in Lude House in the Prince's honour. Her cousin, William Murray, Marquis of Tullibardine, then calling himself Duke William (the Jacobite Duke) asked her to prepare Blair Castle for the Prince's arrival and on 31 August 1745, Lady Lude, 'the very personification of elegance and dignity', stood at the entrance to welcome William and the Royal Prince to whom she was seen to kneel and kiss his hand. The events of this time were chronicled by Commissary Bisset and of Lady Lude he wrote that she 'is here with them, and behaves like a Giglet, and hath taken upon her to be sole mistress of the house [Blair Castle]'.

Lady Lude set herself up as a sort of recruiting sergeant, cajoling the tenants to join the Jacobite army which many were unwilling to do. She then made the threat to them, that if they did not enlist and support the Prince, she would unleash the clans on them and their property would be destroyed. Reluctantly they enlisted, joining a company in Lord George Murray's regiment which became known as Lady Lude's Company. They all deserted during the march to Edinburgh and on arriving back home were each fined £3 by a furious Lady Lude. When Jacobite hopes were finally dashed at Culloden, Lady Lude fled to Edinburgh, where she hid under the name of Mrs Black but she was able to return to Lude following the Act of Indemnity in 1747.

Parish Midwife

An entry in the church heritors' records of 15 November 1764 gives details of assistance provided to the Lude gardener's wife to further her knowledge:

> A petition to the meeting was given in by Louisa Robertson spouse to John Rattray, Gardner at Lude, setting forth that she had attended Doctor Young's lectures on Midwifery in order to qualify her for exercising that business in the parish of Blair Atholl, being put in hopes that the Six Gunieas she paid Dr. Young would be reimbursed by the Kirk Session, and therefore praying the said sum might be allowed her. Which desire the Session finding Reasonable, have granted the same upon the following terms, firstly, that the said Louisa Robertson Exercise Midwifery within their Parish, But not restricting her from giving assistance without the parish, when called; secondly, that in the event of her removing out of the parish within the space of six years, after this date, she shall repay the said sum of Six Gunieas to the Session, and for implementing these conditions, James Robertson, Esq of Lude gave his obligatory missive.

Monzie (hilly place) 906 679 was always one of the principal holdings in the barony and is located on the southern slopes of Carn Liath.

John MacGlashan alias McFergus vic Allaster vic Thomas in Wester Monzie, was accused in the Lude Baron Court on 15 April 1627 of attacking his brother Alex 'in the head with a dirk'. Further, he was accused of twice preventing the enforcing officer, Thomas McInnes of carrying out his duties and was fined £40 Scots.

Charles Robertson and Pat MacGlashan in Easter Monzie, were verbally commissioned by the tenants there in 1723 to purchase a bull. This they did, buying a three-year-old bull at a cost of 20 merks and 40 pence, (£13.4s.0d Scots). When

The ruins of a lime kiln are all that remain of Cairndeshal beside Loch Moraig. Trouble arose over the theft of a ram in the eighteenth century.

Monzie, a large Hill farm on the Lude estate, on the southern slopes of Carn Liath. In 1723 problems arose over the purchase of a bull which the tenants refused to pay for.

the time came for the tenants to pay, they all refused in spite of the complainants' insistence that 'they have had all the benefits of the bull for their cows all the last season having none of their own. . .' and demanded their money. Each tenant was ordered to pay 4 merks (£2.13s 4d) and their proportion of 4 merks for the cost of wintering the bull.

There is hardly any trace of **Cairndeshal** (sunwise cairn) 917 673, on the west side of Loch Moraig. Until 1725 this was pasture land but in that year it was 'selected for improvement' with a number of houses and barns being built for the new tenants. Close by are the remains of an old kiln with the flue still visible. Originally these kilns were used for drying grain by means of sheaves being laid on a grid of branches, which were supported by a ledge built half way up the chamber. A fire was then lit at the outer end of the flue and the ensuing heat dried the grain.

These drying kilns were necessary in areas like upland north Perthshire, when cereal crops were sometimes sown as late as June and not harvested until November, with grinding facilities at the mills being very primitive and lacking means of drying. With agricultural improvements at the end of the eighteenth century bringing better seed, earlier sowing, the prospect of earlier harvesting and with the mills themselves introducing their own drying, these drying kilns fell out of use. Many were converted to burning limestone for fertiliser with the flues being lengthened to increase the draught to give the necessary greater heat.

Theft of a Ram

Alex Macpharlan, a tenant in Cairndeshal, was accused by Grissel McAllan in 1726 of stealing her ram, which was worth about 4 merks (£2.13s 4d Scots). Grissel maintained that:

> . . . After diligent searching there was a great quantity of unsalted mutton and wool found underground in the said defenders house so that the complainer had good ground to suspect that the said defender made use of her ram and

> for further evidence she hath the said ram's horn that was found in the town after 2 days that he was missed. . .

The Baillie found Alex guilty and fined him 4 merks and costs. Alex then confessed to:

> . . . killing a sheep that belonged to his brothers and also that he found 2 in a peat moss which he made use of privately without acquainting any of his neighbours and that the said sheep was not his own.

For this he was fined £4 Scots for the two sheep, £20 Scots as surety for his good behaviour and was told to 'flit and remove immediately from Cairndeshall unless he finds baill [guarantor]. . .'

A small cairn known as the **Fiddler's Cairn** 904 661 lies to the south of Cairndeshal and is in memory of a man who died there on his way to Glen Fender. His name may have been MacDougall as a 1790 plan of the area shows a cairn at this spot called Carnichoul. A little further to the south and across the march dyke with Atholl there is an ancient mound known locally as the **Chief's Grave** 898 649. It stands on a small natural hillock covered with grass and heather and measures 36 feet by 32 feet. It has been much reduced in height to only a few feet and the dug out interior has revealed two side slabs of a cist.

Kenamone (head of peat moss) 915 669 is on the east side of Loch Moraig and was at one time a large settlement. All that remains now is a sheep roundel, lost in the midst of a modern plantation.

On 20 February 1735 Alex MacLauchlan from Kenamone was the subject of a complaint by John Campbell who alleged that MacLauchlan refused to pay him half a sheep, promised in lieu of wages due to John's son. The debt was £3.18s 4d. and Alex was ordered by the court to pay up immediately. Earlier that year, John MacLauchlan had accused Robert Gow of Tomkindrochit of giving him a cow in payment of a horse, promising that if the cow was not in calf he would give him another cow, which he thereafter had refused. Again the court made him fulfil his promise.

Mualichmore Party

The name **Mualichmore** (the big top) 894 675 reflects the situation of the settlement, on the edge of a steep bank caused by glaciation.

George Ritchie was the tenant in 1822, with a three-year lease and paying a rent of £24 a year for

The Mualichmore barn, scene of George Ritchie's party, which was attended by an excise officer.

Kirkton of Lude, a parish church until the 1650s, pictured before the east gable end was taken down for safety reasons.

the farm. He was described by the factor as, 'not a great deal better than his neighbours. Farm tolerably well managed.'

He was summoned to appear before the Dunkeld Excise Court in 1828, charged with selling whisky without a licence at a dance held in his barn. It so happened that one of the revellers was an excise officer who had apparently helped himself to large quantities of liquor and George maintained that surely he must have realised that the whisky had been brought in by the party-goers, pleading that he had nothing to do with the sale of any whisky. He had merely given the use of his barn for the dance, playing his fiddle for the dancing.

The remains of the ancient church we now call **Kirkton of Lude** 903 688 are sited on a level piece of ground above the Fender Burn. There is no precise date for the foundation of this church, but it was a parsonage in the Bagimond Roll, paying a tithe to Rome of 2 merks (£1.6s 8d Scots) a year in 1275, clear proof that it was already an established parish. Sir John Martin who was born in Dunkeld and a capable musician, was its minister in 1514. In 1574, after the Reformation, the reader was a George Mackintosh who was paid £16 Scots a year. This was the church of the Robertson of Lude family until they moved down the glen and after this time it fell into disuse. Up until this period, there were four parishes in the area, St Bride's in Old Blair and Struan which became established Church of Scotland, while Kirkton of Lude and Kilmaveonaig became Episcopalian and remained as such.

An open-air service at Kirkton of Lude in July 1989.

Brae of Lude 901 690 sits up the hill a few hundred yards above the old church, near the main glen track. At a meeting of the Kirk Session in Blair Atholl on 18 January 1761:

> . . . There was an Application made to the session on behalf of Alex McLauchlane in Brae of Lude who had his horse in harvest last killed by a thunder-clap, he hardly escaping himself being just beside the said horse, for a collection to be made at both the churches in this parish, in order to help him in buying another, to keep him from being a burden upon the parish. . .

The following year the Kirk Session records show that on 10 January:

> . . . John McLauchlane in Brae of Lude was fined in two shillings sterling for being too late in coming at his daughter's marriage, of which one shilling sterling, was given to Rachel Cameron in Toldunie and the other shilling sterling , was left with himself to give to any poor object he sees most useful. . .

Aldandulish (black/grey little stream) 905 692 stands on a knoll above the Fender Burn and is the topmost settlement in the glen. Donald Stewart took up the lease of the farm in 1834, only to discover that the houses 'were so unsuitable that he rebuilt all except one which he hopes to do when his lease is renewed'. He also requested that a stackyard enclosed by a dyke should be built as his farm was 'the highest in the glen and exposed to all cattle and sheep in the hill which damage his corn'. Aldandulish was inhabited until well into this century, but has become a ruin once more. Locally, the place is called 'Burn Douglas' showing how easily and mistakenly a Gaelic place name can be misinterpreted.

The settlement stands beside **Allt Glac Sheillich** (stream of the hollow of the willow) which runs into the Fender. Here the place name would indicate that willow trees must once have been in abundance, although none are growing now. The willow was a very valued tree in the Highlands in the past and was put to endless uses. No part of it was wasted as the bark was used in tanning leather, while its foliage was acceptable

Brae of Lude, the home of John McLauchlan who was fined in 1762 for being late at his daughter's wedding.

Craig Choinnich Lodge built by Colonel McInroy in the 1820s.

fodder for cattle and horses. The young twigs were employed in basket work and even in rope making.

The shooting lodge called **Craig Choinnich** (mossy crag) 919 703 stands on a rocky outcrop on the east bank of the Fender. It was built by Colonel William McInroy (who purchased the Lude estate from the Robertsons of Lude in 1821) for use in times of stalking and grouse shooting, and later, a cart road was made to link it with Lude House.

Cromalltan Pass

Aldvialich (stream of the pass) 919 715 was the highest shieling in the glen and had over twenty bothies astride the stream. The 'Pass' refers to the Cromalltan Pass which is the easiest way of crossing the Beinn a' Ghlo mountains, between Carn Liath and Braigh Coire Chruinn-bhalgain. The route climbed to 2,440 feet (750m) and the pass itself is just half a mile in length as it goes between the mountains.

The Duke of Atholl owned the top of Carn Liath, while Lude possessed the sides to the point where 'water rises'. This meant that a narrow tongue of Atholl land projected southwards for more than a mile, but as the land at each end of the pass belonged to Lude, his tenants in Glen Fender used the pass when taking their livestock to the market in Kirkmichael, thus cutting out a circuit of five to six miles round Carn Liath and on by the Shinagag road.

In 1839 a great bonfire was built to celebrate the 6th Duke's wedding, when wood and tar barrels were driven up the pass to the top of Carn Liath. Another bonfire was lit there in 1861 to celebrate the coming of age of the 7th Duke and both these celebrations had the effect of widening the track.

A dispute arose in 1888 as to whether the Cromalltan Pass was a right of way, the Atholl keepers challenging the Lude keepers and accusing them of trespassing. Lude insisted that he had a right to use the pass, and in an apparent effort to avoid litigation, the 7th Duke offered to allow McInroy and his tenants to use it during the first month of the grouse shooting season, provided they kept off it for the rest of the year! This offer, perhaps not surprisingly, was refused, with Lude claiming not only his own rights, but also those of a public right of way and so the matter went to law.

John Young, a civil engineer and architect from Perth, was called on by Lude to testify. He said that the path was very distinct and varied in width from two to four feet and from its appearance he thought it was very old. It was well defined and well trodden, bearing clear marks of usage and was a road along which men and horses could go with ease. He was of the opinion however, that the track itself had not been made by man and that it did not resemble a drove road but rather one which had been worn away by the feet of men and ponies. An unexpected witness was the Rev. Donald Cameron, a minister in the Canadian Presbyterian Church, who said that he had often gone to the head of the pass with a horse and cart and felt sure that three men abreast could travel up it.

The judge in the case found that there was no public right of way, but that Lude and his tenants had established a right from unchallenged usage over many years. The Duke at once appealed and the case came before the Inner House when the judgment was reversed. Mr McInroy was not satisfied and appealed to the House of Lords, where in September 1891 his appeal was dismissed, with costs, in favour of the Duke.

Nowadays the track is very indistinct in the lower parts, especially on the eastern side. The western apprpoach is firm and although there are traces of a track, these are intermittent and do not form an established route. The top of the pass is firm and dry and there is much evidence of several tracks, made more likely by sheep and deer than by man.

Aldvialich and the Cromalltan Pass, subject of a right of way case in 1888.

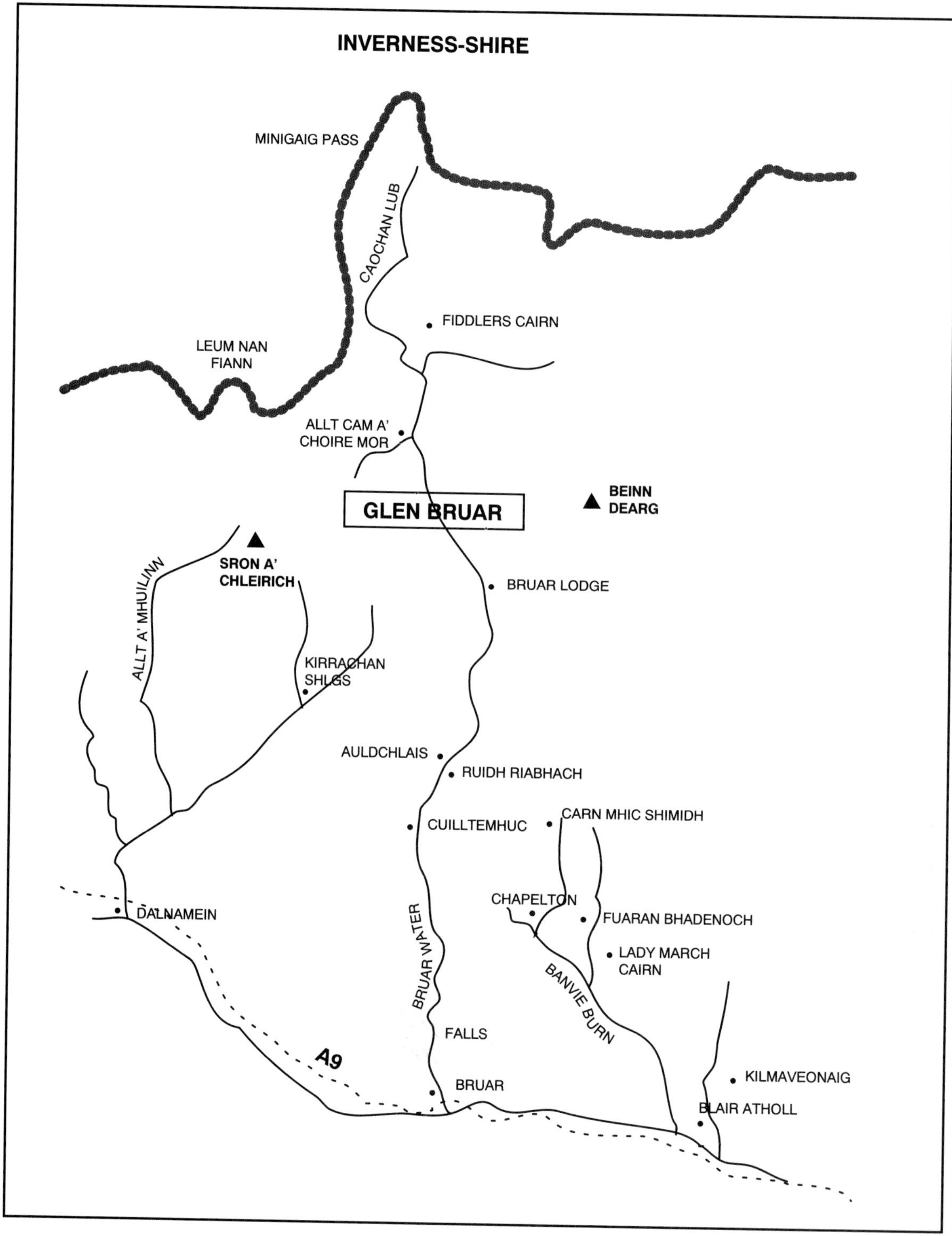
INVERNESS-SHIRE
MINIGAIG PASS
CAOCHAN LUB
FIDDLERS CAIRN
LEUM NAN FIANN
ALLT CAM A' CHOIRE MOR
GLEN BRUAR
BEINN DEARG
SRON A' CHLEIRICH
ALLT A' MHUILINN
BRUAR LODGE
KIRRACHAN SHLGS
AULDCHLAIS
RUIDH RIABHACH
CUILLTEMHUC
CARN MHIC SHIMIDH
CHAPELTON
FUARAN BHADENOCH
DALNAMEIN
LADY MARCH CAIRN
BRUAR WATER
BANVIE BURN
FALLS
A9
BRUAR
KILMAVEONAIG
BLAIR ATHOLL

CHAPTER SIX

GLEN BRUAR

The Bruar Water joins the Garry about four miles west of Blair Atholl. It runs through a glen about twelve miles in length, much of it bleak and uncompromising and in its lower parts the water is for the most part, reduced to a meagre trickle in its rocky bed, mainly due to the existence of a hydro-electric dam which has diverted most of it elsewhere.

The most famous shooting tenant of Bruar Lodge in its early days was William Scrope who rented it for ten years from 1824 and described the glen thus:

> About eight reputed miles north of Blair Atholl, which distance could be numbered ten in a county of milestones, you descend into a glen, which is of a wild and desolate character. The heather being old, is rather of a brown colour; but there is some relief of greensward near the lodge, and more in various patches near the winding course of the Bruar. Huge, lofty and in the district of Atholl second only in magnitude to Ben-y-Gloe, Ben Dearg or the red mountain, stands dominant. . . Down winds the Bruar through the glen, sometimes creeping silently through the mossy stones, at others raving maddening and bearing all before it. Nearby in front of the lodge is a wooden foot bridge raised high above the water so as to give it free passage. Some distance up the glen, towards the east, a lofty cataract falls from the mountain side and the head of the glen is obstructed by a chain of mountains.

It was the old Minigaig Pass route through the Grampians from Blair Atholl to Badenoch that brought prosperity to Glen Bruar and along its length at one time were settlements and shielings. The opening of the military road through Glen Garry and over Drumochter deprived the glen of its main sources of income and gave impetus to its population decline, so that today, apart from the keeper and his wife living at Bruar Lodge, the glen is deserted.

Wild and desolate Glen Bruar with Bruar Lodge a mere 'speck' below the upland Grampian plateau.

As controversy had arisen in Parliament and the newspapers about the amount of land large landowners were setting aside for sporting purposes, Lord Tullibardine (later the 8th Duke) decided to try to counter this by setting up the Tullibardine Commission in 1909. A committee made up from working men of varying political persuasions led by two barristers rode up Glen Bruar on horseback in 1909 to the top of **Ben Dearg** (red mountain) 853 778, and round the hill to Forest Lodge in Glen Tilt. So confident was 'Bardie', as Lord Tullibardine, the 7th Duke's eldest son was known, of the findings of the committee, that he offered one of the delegates, Alexander Gow, a Dundee shuttle-maker, a free gift of any land he discovered in the deer forest which would make a suitable small-holding. Promising sites were frequently seen, but which on closer inspection turned out to be moss, many inches deep, with little or no loam beneath.

The findings of the Commission were unanimous:

1. That the area comprised in the Deer Forest of Atholl consists wholly of high barren and mountainous land, the surface of which is composed chiefly of peat, bog and stone;
2. That the land in the said Forest has never been used as agricultural land in the past;
3. That the said land is in every way unsuitable for small holdings or any such like agricultural purpose;
4. That it would be impracticable to utilise the said area for sheep farming or timber planting;
5. And that on the other hand the utilisation of the said area as a deer forest appears to be the best use to which this area can be put, from the point of view of the owners, inasmuch as it provides a larger volume of direct and indirect employment than any alternative which has been suggested.

Bruar's appearance in the military history of Scotland took place in 1746, just before the Battle of Culloden. As the Jacobite army retreated towards Inverness in February, the Duke of Cumberland stationed five hundred men from the Argyllshire Highlanders, mainly Campbells' in the Atholl district, in Struan, Blair Castle, Blair Inn, Bridge of Tilt, Lude House and Blairfettie. When Lord George Murray heard this, he gathered together a force of seven hundred men and quickly arrived at Dalnaspidal, where he divided them into parties which were to attack the various posts held by the enemy, while he went to Bruar to await their return.

Blair Castle was garrisoned by Sir Andrew Agnew for the government, who sent out a party of troops to apprehend Lord George who was caught unawares, having only twenty four men with him, but rejecting any thought of surrender, he gathered his meagre force behind a turf wall, spacing them out. He then gave orders for them to display their colours and instructed his pipers to play 'their most boisterous pibroch', whilst the rest were to brandish their broadswords aggressively. The approaching arrest party 'after listening for half a minute to the tumult of bagpipes, and casting a brief glimpse at the glittering broadswords, turned back'.

At this time, Bruar and the settlements around, were part of the Brae Lands of Faskally and came under the jurisdiction of the Faskally Baron Court. Donald Stewart, from nearby Calbruar, accused Donald Robertson at the 'Miln of Bruar', in the court, that on the last day of February 1715, he:

> . . . came under silence of night to my house with a drawn dirk in his hand and finding he could not break the door up, went up to the roof of my house endeavouring to come in through the roof and finding difficulty there, he came down, whereupon I opened the door and made my escape and left the door wide open. By all which the said Donald Robertson is guilty of ill neighbourhood and ought to be punished. . .

The Baillie at the court fined Donald Robertson and ordered his goods to the amount owed to be poinded.

Corn Mill Complaints

The Bruar corn mill was sited below the present road bridge and all traces have gone. As with most mills, there were plenty of causes for irritation, anger and sometimes recourse to law between the miller and tenants. In 1739 a number of complaints were made about John Strong, the miller, especially concerning the quality of his grinding:

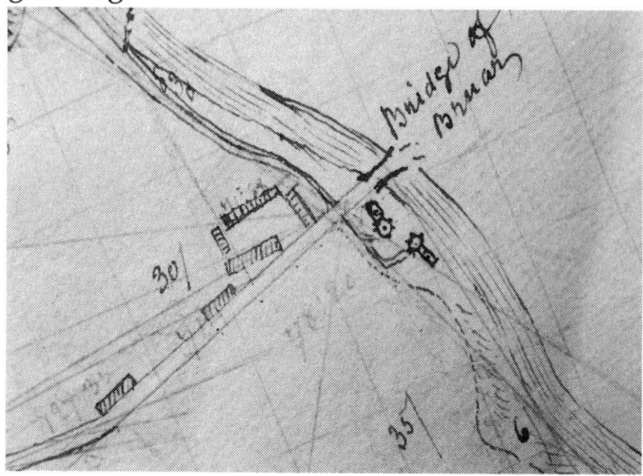

A 1790 plan of Bruar. The two water mills are shown below the bridge, the corn mill being nearer the road.

> 20th March 1739
> John Strong confesses that he did grind a bag of white oat shilling [grain freed from the husks] to James Stewart in Clunes, too great and that it was returned to him about Candlemas last [2 February] and that he grinded it again, but says

the corn was not enough dryed which was the reason for the bad grinding. . .

John Forbes in Clunes complains that he came over after Whitsunday last with half a boll of dry bear [barley] to the miln and desired prompt grinding. The miller answered he could not stay to grind to him that day because he was obliged to be in his father in law's peats, who was a poor widower, neither could he promise the miln graith [machinery] was sufficient enough to set the mill agrinding and leave it with the complainer who was pledged that he must have his stuff [grain] grinded before he would return home because his wife was bedfast at home and he wanted [needed] meall. But if the miller would. . . set the mill agrinding he would wait on it himself, which the miller did and left the miln grinding and when it was about half done, some aws [buckets] of the cut[t]er wheel broke and the complainer put off the water and sett the mill and with the assistance of the miller's wife (when he could get nobody that would run for him to the moss to fetch the miller) he took the stuff that remained unground out of the hopper into his sack again, carry'd away the meall home and when he came next day he got the remainder grind and ready for him. . .

John Fergusson in Dalreoch complains that in Summer 1737 he came with some dry bear to the miln and that the milner told him when he desired grinding that his mistress [proprietor] was sending him to the wood and if she would allow him to stay he would grind it to him, but that Mrs Stewart told him she could not dispense with him that day and that the miln was left grinding by the milner's wife and that his meall was too round. . .

A number of tenants complained that they:

. . . have not only been hindered at the said miln and made to come several times to get their stuff grind but must return without it and when they expostilate with the said miller for making them travel often in rain, he not only answered saucily and impertinently, without giving them any other satisfaction and beat some of the servants belonging to the tennants of the suiken [area thirled to a mill]. . . and therefore the said defenders ought and should. . . repair the skaith [machinery]. . . and the said John Strong to be removed from his office against next term and Mrs Stewart ordained to provide a sufficient miller to serve the suiken as becomes in time coming.

The court sustained 'the Clame relevant and admits the same to the pursuers probation.'

Distillery Plans

A lint mill for processing flax, to be powered by the same water supply, was built below the corn mill in 1790. The growing and production of flax fell as quickly as it had risen in this part of the Highlands, and by 1820, mainly because of cheap imports, many of these mills were being phased out. About this time a proposal was put forward by some tenants for converting the old lint mill into a distillery:

The neighbourhood suffers from want of a market for its produce. Many tenants had barley out of hand which they could not sell and were tempted to turn to smuggling with ruinous consequences. If a distillery were to be erected at Bruar where fine water was available and fuel to be had, and a suitable road, this would be of great assistance. Would the Duke grant timber for building of the necessary buildings and advance £200, half to be paid off in instalments and 5% interest on the remainder.

An 1870s photograph of the railway bridge over the Bruar beside the Falls of Bruar Cottage, now slated.

The 'Stone of Sacrifice' near the former Falls of Bruar Hotel. Two hundred years ago this large stone was in the centre of a circle of smaller stones.

> There is always a plentiful supply of fine water from the Bruar, the road passes it and the fuel which is a natural object to a distiller is not difficult to be had.
>
> We humbly suggest that as lint is not now so used or so much of it sown in the countryside as formerly, that money intended to be laid out by Your Grace on the erection of a lint mill, might be advantageously laid out on a distillery. Besides the wall of the present lint mill will serve for a still house.

The scheme was rejected and by the mid 1830s both mills had ceased to operate. By this time the Falls of Bruar were becoming more widely known and the farmhouse was converted into an inn to accommodate some of the many travellers who had come to admire them. With the arrival of the railway in 1863, the inn closed and reverted back to being a farmhouse for a hundred years, as it reopened as the Falls of Bruar Hotel in 1963, closing its doors for the last time in January 1992, prior to a proposed major redevelopment.

Falls of Bruar

Upstream are the series of falls which combine to make up the famous Falls of Bruar. Visitors in the eighteenth century saw a very different scene of bare, open hillside, awesome in its forbidding, rocky desolation, until the trees were planted.

In 1787 Robert Burns set out on his only tour of the Highlands and stayed in Blair Castle as a

Rustic view house overlooking the Falls of Bruar in 1810. (Sketch by Lady Emily Murray)

Lower Falls of Bruar in 1810. (Sketch by Lady Emily Murray)

Upper Falls of Bruar in 1810. (Sketch by Lady Emily Murray)

guest of the 4th Duke. He paid a visit to the falls and afterwards wrote the *Humble Petition of Bruar Water to the Duke of Atholl*, where he adopts the guise of the river and requests that the Duke should plant the bare banks with trees and verse five seems to capture the poet's sentiments:

Would, then, my noble master please
To grant my highest wishes?
He'll shade my banks wi' tow'ring trees,
And bonie spreading bushes.
Delighted doubly then, my Lord,
You'll wander on my banks,
And listen mony a grateful bird
Return you tuneful thanks.

Robert Burns died in 1796 with his pleas for Bruar unfulfilled and it was only after his death, ten years after his visit, that the Duke was spurred into action. Within a few months, 60,000 larch and an equal number of Scotch pines were planted and less than a year after the poet's death a new wild garden was created in his memory. A number of view houses were erected beside the path, from which the best views of the falls could be obtained and by 1844 and Queen Victoria's visit, the trees were mature and Burns' objections to the bare hillside removed.

At the time of the Queen's visit in September 1844, the falls were at their spectacular best after several days of heavy rain. Both she and Albert were enchanted with the views as is shown in her diary:

> . . . At every turn the view of the rushing water is extremely fine, and looking back the hills, which are so clear and so beautifully lit up with the rapid stream below, was most exquisite. . .

Cuilltemhuc (pig's nook) 816 713 where a single storey slated house stands, is four miles up the glen and was home to my favourite character. Living here over a hundred years ago was the 'laughing Man of Cuilltemhuc' who was found, blind drunk, in a water trough, laughing his head off! No one has ever discovered the subject of his merriment, whisky excepted!

Cuilltemhuc is beside the eight-mile track to Bruar Lodge and it was near here that Thomas Christie,

Charles Christie, who performed the Sword Dance before Queen Victoria in 1842, as a sergeant in the Atholl Highlanders in 1893. His father had a fatal accident on the Bruar track in 1821.

a carpenter at Blair Castle, had a tragic accident in 1821. At that time he had been staying in Bruar Lodge and was travelling down the glen on top of a cartload of furniture, when he fell off. His leg became jammed between the wheel and the cart, dragging him along for a considerable way before he was able to extricate himself. Eventually, Charles Fraser, a farm servant who had been with Christie, noticed that he was missing and retraced the route for several miles, finding him in a 'miserable state'. It was dark by the time they reached Blair Atholl and only then was the seriousness of the injuries discovered. The leg bones were shattered and the mangled leg was dressed, to the best of his ability, by Dr Stewart, who declared it was the worst case of its kind that he had ever seen. Sadly Thomas Christie died within four weeks of his terrible ordeal.

Thomas Christie's father John had also been a carpenter at Blair Castle. At the Battle of Killiecrankie, 'Bonnie' Dundee was supposed to have sustained the fatal shot under his arm, but his breast-plate, now in Blair Castle, bears a hole through the middle and the story goes that the 4th Duke, in order to give the breast -plate a more warlike and battle-scarred appearance, instructed John Christie to make the hole in it! On the 4th Duke's death he received an annuity of £20. His grandson Charles, the unfortunate Thomas's son, entered the service of Duchess Marjory, the second wife of the 4th Duke, as a footman in 1834. He performed the sword dance before Queen Victoria at Dunkeld in 1842, 'displaying great alacrity and expertness in executing the steps'.

Comyn's Road

There is an old tradition that after the Red Comyn had built Comyn's Tower in 1269, the forerunner to the present castle, he and his wife were passing through Atholl and on arrival in the small village of Kilmaveonaig, went to the inn for refreshment. They quickly ordered more of the ale which was made on the premises, liking its taste and quality so much that they asked the landlord where the ingredients came from. He told them there was nothing special about the malt which came from Perth, but that it was the water from a little stream, which still flows past the church, that gave his ale its special taste and flavour. There and then the great man resolved to transport the ale across the trackless hills of the Grampians to his other castle at Ruthven in Badenoch, 26 miles to the north.

After surveying the ground, he drew a line from Kilmaveonaig, through Craig Urrard, crossed the Bruar near Ruichlachrie and Cuilltemhuc and on in a straight line till it reached Gaick and then Ruthven five miles further on. Whether the story of his desire for Atholl ale led directly to his building the road that bears his name is true, or not, we do not know. What is certain, however, is that a highway called **Rathad nan Cuimenach** (Comyn's Road) existed between Atholl and Ruthven for many centuries.

Fate of Walter Comyn

It was in a desolate place that Lord Walter Comyn, a relative of the Red Comyn, met a terrible end at **Leum nan Fiann** (Fingalians' Leap) 773 805, near the county march. An old manuscript describes his fate:

> . . . He ended miserablie being torn in pieces with a hors in Badenoch, whair, falling from his hors, his fut stak in the stirrop and was brocht to Blair by the said hors. . .

Walter had decreed that all the women of Badenoch between the ages of twelve and thirty years should work naked in the harvest fields in Ruthven and he was returning on horseback to ensure that his vile orders were being carried out, when retribution overtook him. His horse was at last found at Leth-Chois in Glen Tilt (see page 71) and when a search was made, his mangled body was discovered beside the road at Leum nan Fiann, with two eagles preying on it. Comyn's gory end was attributed to the supernatural, with the eagles representing two of the mothers of the harvest girls. It is still a desolate, awesome place and a centuries' old curse - 'Walter's fate of Gaick on you' recalls his terrible ending.

The start of Comyn's Road was from Kilmaveonaig, crossing the Tilt by the Priest's Ford opposite and then ascending up the south side of the Banvie Burn, across which was an extensive settlement called **Bail an t'Sepail** (Chapelton) 840 696. Although no trace of the chapel has been found, the remains of at least

Lady March Cairn, scene of a picnic with the 7th Duke.

fourteen buildings are clearly visible in a large area of cleared ground.

On a cold, dark night in 1723, disaster struck one the tenants, Donald Stewart:

> 10th November 1723
> The bearer, Donald Steward in Riechapel [Chapelton] above Blair Atholl is come of honest parents, a married man free of all public scandals or church censure having behaved honestly and civilly, had his barn and all his corn and most part of his bed clothes lying in that large barn burnt up quite by accidental fire in the dead time of night, carried thither by violence of the wind, sixth of this current month, by which loss he is rendered a great object of pity and charity of all tender hearted Christians who may know that he is an honest tenant but of no considerable stock, almost all his all being lost except the person and his family. . .

The Atholl estate reacted promptly to Donald's distress and reduced his rent by £12 Scots. At least six families were living in Chapelton throughout the eighteenth century and it was inhabited until around 1850.

About a mile away to the south east there is a prominent cairn called **Lady March Cairn** 852 691 which stands six feet tall and was built in the last century when the 7th Duke had a picnic there with Lady March. She started a small cairn and workmen repairing the West Hand track nearby, built it much larger. Below the cairn on the steep bank above Allt na Moine Baine there is a partly chiselled millstone still lying in the ground. The hole in the centre has been outlined but a great flaw in one edge rendered the stone useless and it was abandoned.

The incomplete mill stone below Lady March Cairn.

Minigaig Pass

The Minigaig Pass superseded Comyn's Road by the seventeenth century to become the main route through the Grampians from Atholl and it passes close by Lady March Cairn before joining up with the West Hand road. The Minigaig started from St Bride's church in Old Blair, climbed through the trees to the north of the Banvie and left the West Hand track at a beautifully-shaped round well called **Fuaran Bhadenoch** (Well of Badenoch) 844 708, which is 2 feet 6 inches in diameter, skilfully lined with stones and marked with a vertical stone slab. There were countless wells of this sort beside the old highways, which were often provided with a stone cup for passing travellers to quench their thirst.

Frasers' Cairn

The Minigaig track is clear in the heather as it reaches **Carn Mhic Shimidh** (Frasers' Cairn) 838 723, a mile distant, which was partly damaged by vandals in 1971.

Hundreds of years ago, when the men of Atholl were away - possibly on a raid of their own - a band of Frasers, under their chief who revelled in plunder and pillage, invaded Atholl on a looting expedition. As they were returning home along the Minigaig road with their booty, Donald Fraser, a member of the party, heard a cock crowing in a nearby farm. He reminded the chief that he had sworn that he would leave 'neither horses, cattle nor sheep, not even domestic fowls alive' and acknowledging this, he sent off a small party, led by Donald Fraser, to despatch the offending cockerel.

In the meantime the Atholl men had returned, raised the alarm and, encountering the small band of Frasers, killed them all except Donald, who was a powerful man, fighting vigorously before he was overcome and kept as a hostage. He managed to make his escape over the moor, but was caught and also slain. A number of the Atholl men then dressed in the Fraser men's plaids and proceeded slowly to join up with the main party of Frasers waiting further up the track. This gave time for a much larger group of Atholl men to go

The Well of Badenoch beside the old Minigaig Pass route.

round by the Bruar, get behind the Frasers and at a given signal, attack the enemy from both the front and the rear, quickly winning the day. The spot where this skirmish took place is marked by the cairn, the Fraser chief being killed while calling for his horse.

Frasers' Cairn is associated with the last sighting of the witch of Beinn a' Ghlo. The story goes that two men went poaching in Glen Tarf when they were overtaken by a blizzard and were forced eventually to seek shelter in a shieling bothy which turned out to be inhabited by an old women of wild and haggard appearance. She had large, ugly features, long, lank, dishevelled hair and deep-set, piercing grey eyes, and so fearful were these men of her, that they could hardly eat the food she prepared for them. When she discovered that they had brought no venison with them, she told them, that to make amends, they had to leave a fat stag at midnight on the first Monday of every month, beside Frasers' Cairn. Then in a fear-inspiring rage, she warned them that if they failed, a terrible fate would befall them and that their 'banes shall be pickit by the eagle'.

About a mile up river are the remains of a shieling called **Ruidh Riabhach** (brindled shieling) 823 725 which eventually became a permanent settlement, with people living there until 1800.

In November 1757 a petition was lodged with the 2nd Duke, by Gregor McEwan, 'Your Grace's tenant of Rie Riach, a new possession in Glen Bruar':

> . . . Humbly sheweth, that when one Macklauchlane having taken a tack of Rie Riach for a new possession, as Gregor Murray and Patrick McGlashan thought their sheallings prejudged thereby, they contrived his ruin by an alledgence of his killing deer. That after I took a tack of that same possession from your Grace, I was told that I Behooved to court Patk. Mackglashan's friendship or I might expect the same treatment, and therefore I was making presents to him to the value of a crown yearly, whereof, your Grace being informed, I was discharged to own Patk. Mackglashan any more, but to pay the addition of the crown yearly to my rent, which I have done. But ever since, he, Patrick has been plotting against me, first by outhounding constables from time to time to seize upon my own support, a son of mine, who in my old age manages my farm, altho' he is not fitt for the army, being much under size, and refused the other year on that account when impressed; and now, to crown all, he has got two of his creatures, the two Toschachs, to accuse me of Deer Killing, altho' they are notour Deer Killers themselves, carrying guns and dogs to the Forrest for that end; and one of them, who was servant to Mr Mackglashan, was so far assisted by him that he sent north for a Deerkilling dog which he keeped for his use, and allowed the use of him from time to time to the Forrest, and now thinks to get himself indemnifyed for accusing and witnessing against me, as was done formerly to one of those Toschachs, a notour Deer Killer, for informing that he had given a piece venison to Gregor Murray's wife, which was done in revenge of his hightning the rent of the Miln of Blair and taking it over the Mackglashans' heads; and as I find my possession is the bone of contention and that I can neither have peace nor safey until I give it up.

Poor Gregor McEwan never had a chance. As soon as the Duke found out he was bribing Patrick, he added the value of his bribe to the rent and when he was accused of poaching deer by two men who were renowned for it themselves, he could stand it no more and appealed to the Duke. In the end, Patrick Mackglashan had the satisfaction of seeing Gregor depart and of taking over his lease.

Bruar Lodge

Bruar Lodge in 1860 before considerable alterations were carried out. William Scrope leased the lodge in the 1820s with a glowing reference from Sir Walter Scott.

Eight miles up the glen the track comes to **Bruar Lodge** 832 761. The original lodge was situated two miles further on but was rebuilt on its present site in 1789 and called **Cabar Feith** (deer's antler). Its most famous tenant, William Scrope, who had a ten-year lease from 1824, was recommended to the Duke by Sir Walter Scott as an 'Englishman of family and fortune':

> I am enabled to say that Mr Scrope is not only a perfect gentleman, and incapable of indulging his love of sport otherwise that as becomes one, but that he is a man of highly cultivated taste and understanding as well as much accomplishments.

This glowing reference secured for William Scrope a long association with the Atholl area and that same summer he rented Bruar Lodge for the first time. The Duke regarded him as a kind of amateur head keeper, as he kept Blair Castle supplied with grouse and venison, occasionally sending haunches of venison to his friends.

He gives a graphic description of Bruar Lodge in the 1820s:

> At the right entrance to the pass, the little white and lonely dwelling called Bruar Lodge, lies a mere speck beneath it. It consists of two small tenements facing each other, encompassed by a wall so as to form a court between them. One of these buildings serves the master and the other for his servants. There is besides, a lodging for the hill-men, rather frail in structure, and a dog kennel of the same picturesque character. Close by stands a black stack of peats.

Poaching Incident

Two miles up-river, on the west bank are the remains of six shieling bothies which formed the shieling of **Allt Cam a' Choire Mor** (crooked burn of the great corrie) 817 790, which was leased at the end of the eighteenth century to the Blair minister, the Rev. James McLagan. In 1807 the Bruar keepers were involved in a poaching incident:

> On Tuesday 30th September 1807, Charles Frazer and Robert Crerar heard a shot on the Bruar side and saw 2 men at a deer on the Cammocharre of Bruar which they were drawing up the hillside and then covering with heather. John Crerar sent Charles Frazer and John McMillan to secure the deer and catch the poachers. They went to the bothy at Cammocharre and found Alex McDonald shepherd to Mr Mitchell, Tacksman in Guaick. He was charged with killing the deer and denied it. They went to the place where the deer was hidden and Mr McDonald went home to Guaick. They returned to the bothy for the night, intending to take the deer to Glen Bruar the next morning. When they arrived at the place, the deer had gone so they travelled to Guaick and Mr McDonald admitted that he had shot the deer and that it was carried to Badenoch to a person whose name he would not mention.

This was a remarkable feat of strength and endurance to carry a deer at night, a distance of nearly eight miles across wild and intractable country, where for much of the way there was barely a path. The bothy that the keepers spent the night in was used until the start of this century to prevent poaching and became known as the 'Watchers' Bothy'.

It is four miles from Bruar Lodge to the head of the glen at **Uchd na h-Analach** (breathless slope) 819 805 which makes a formidable obstacle on the old Minigaig track which is clearly visible on it, swinging round to the right and mounting the steep slope to climb 500 feet to the top. Once up the slope the unique feature of the Grampians becomes apparent, as this is the start of a three-mile plateau at a height of over 2,500 feet.

Fiddler's Cairn on the Grampian plateau.

At the south end of this plateau there is a fine s1x-foot cairn called **Fiddler's Cairn** 815 819, standing on top of **Uchd a' Chlarsair** (harper's upland). The **Caochan Lub shieling** (meandering stream) 810 820 is located a few hundred yards north of the cairn.

On 24 June 1696 Aeneas Macpherson from Killihuntly in Badenoch wrote to the Marquis of Atholl informing him that he was 'straitened for want of hill grass' and asking permission to pasture his cattle in this shieling. The request was granted, but by 1704 the Atholl factor was checking up on his tenants and recorded:

> . . . It is said he keeps a great many cattle there not only in his own name but under the name of Bowmen, who sheall thereon likewise, and that this year he will have about 57 head of cattle. It is informed that he kills a great many deer in the forests having hired of late the best deer-stalkers in the two countries.

Following this, Aeneas was restricted to pasturing no more than thirty to forty head of cattle on the shieling and also had to promise that his men would stop hunting deer with guns and dogs.

Minigaig Summit

The summit of the Minigaig Pass is reached at a height of 2,745 feet (845m) at the **Coire Bhran** (raven's corrie) 812 847 from where the view right across to Speyside, Kingussie and beyond, is spectacular.

In winter the Minigaig had a savage reputation, claiming many victims. There is the tale of a company of soldiers losing their lives in a violent storm when marching over the pass on their way to the barracks at Ruthven in 1745. The Blair Atholl Kirk Session minutes for 13 October 1777 recorded:

> . . . the Session appointed 16 shillings sterling for coffins and dead cloths for the two women that were lost upon a rapid burn this side of Minigaig, going back to the North from Lothian shearing [harvest]. . .

The danger of the supernatural was also present. **Sithean** (fairy knolls) are numerous, while **Chon Dubh** (black dog) was a name of evil omen. The combination of these two elements in **Sith a Choin Dubh** (fairy hill of the black dog) gives rise to all kinds of sinister connotations and relates in one instance to a sixteenth century Perthshire practice when the Clan MacGregor was proscribed and some of their enemies carried this persecution to such lengths that they had a specially trained breed of dogs for seeking their quarry out of their hiding places in the hills. Apparently they did this by rearing the puppies on the milk of MacGregor women so that they would learn to react to the smell of a MacGregor and hunt him down!

Cattle Drovers

During the early part of the nineteenth century, the Minigaig route down Glen Bruar became favoured by cattle drovers seeking to avoid payment of the tolls which were levied on the parliamentary road through Drumochter. The Coire Bhran was the meeting place for drovers for the north of Scotland, who would congregate here and pass through Atholl as a formidable body of men and livestock.

The tollman at the County March in Drumochter reported in 1829 that at least 300 cattle and some horses were passing through Glen Bruar and the drover was encouraging others to follow his example. In September of that year news came that 592 head of cattle had travelled through the glen in three days and memoranda of the time show the concern this caused the Atholl estate:

> 15th June 1829
> There should be no difficulty in stopping them and the Minigaig could easily be closed to drovers. If a few were charged half a merk each for trespassing, they would soon find another route. No drove can claim the right either of driving through a hill such as Minigaig or to lie on the grass for the night.

But some of the Atholl keepers in Glen Bruar were actively encouraging drovers by selling them whisky which was sometimes paid for by them giving presents to the wives and children.

Commenting on all this, the Atholl factor, Frederick Graham wrote:

> Memorandum Blair 10 July 1829
> Referring to John McGrigor's letter to Mr

> Mitchell regarding evasions of Tolls by drovers passing from Inverness-shire by Minegeg, Glenbruar, Glenbanvie and to Tummel Bridge through Invervack - In consequence of a similar complaint about six or seven years ago, Alex Stewart the late Ground Officer was sent up to challenge drovers passing into Glenbruar from the North. Two of the drovers so challenged were William Stewart Kilmaveonag and Charles Stewart now residing about Moulin. They as well as others refused to turn when challenged, saying they were entitled to use it as a public road. They were then counted in case the droves should be attempted to be allowed to remain on the Grass, but this does not appear to have been done, and for this reason no fine appears to have been exacted.
>
> During the times of drovers passing, the Ground Officer is two or three times at least every week up Glenbruar, and has never known an instance of drovers laying or stopping on the Ground, although they cannot avoid straggling a little off the road. The Ground Officer says that since Peter McLaren the forrester went to Glenbruar (when Mr Scrope first took the shooting) there has been no whisky sold by him, and there is no other person to do so.
>
> Duncan Robertson the Tenant at Invervack says he has always challenged droves going to Tummel Bridge through Invervack, and in order to establish the interruption, he has frequently exacted 6d per score when he permitted them to pass, but he allows none to pass on any account between seed time and harvest.
>
> Inquiry will be made how far it may be competent to interrupt droves at Menegeg - and in the mean time, as it can do no harm, Peter McLaren is directed to challenge and count Droves and report with the names of the drovers and by whom employed - he is also directed, if he cannot turn the droves, to prevent them from stopping, and to be very strict in exacting fines if possible for stragglers off the road. . .

The Minigaig Pass continued to be used by drovers until about 1900.

A small drove of cattle.

George Duncan Robertson, eighteenth chief of Clan Donnachaidh, seen here in 1863, the year before his death. He was a lieutenant in the 42nd Highlanders and was described as a man with a 'fine and imposing physique'.

Mary Stewart Menzies, daughter of Major Archibald Menzies, married the eighteenth chief of Clan Donnachaidh in 1839.

CHAPTER SEVEN

GLEN ERROCHTY

Glen Errochty (see map on page 26) is ten miles in length and the river flows due east to join the river Garry at Old Struan. It was the heartland of the Robertsons, or Clan Donnachaidh, whose chief had his lands formed into the free Barony of Struan by a royal charter in 1451.

The main approach to the glen from the east is by Calvine where the Garry is crossed by a single arched stone bridge built in the 1760s. This bridge was right in the way of the Inverness and Perth Junction Railway Company's proposed line from Perth to Inverness, and they surmounted the problem by building a viaduct over the road bridge. The line opened in 1863, but by 1899 an ugly metal bridge was tacked on to the first railway bridge when the track was doubled.

Struan means 'place of streams', reflecting its location at the confluence of the Garry and Errochty rivers. The area of ground at the confluence was called **Socach Struan** 808 653, 'socach' being the Gaelic word for a ploughshare, indicating the shape of the land here, between the rivers. Errochty means 'an assembly' or 'court of justice'. In the past these were often to be found near river confluences and thus shows the importance of Struan in earlier times.

One of the early strongholds of the Clan Donnachaidh chiefs was at **Tom an Tigh Mhor** (knoll of the great house) 807 654, an artificial mound, 30 feet high and 60 feet across its top, near the church and overlooking the Garry. It was a defensive structure with one side protected by a precipitous slope to the Garry, and a dry moat on the other sides.

Inverness and Perth Junction Railway Company's plan showing the railway viaduct crossing the River Garry above the road bridge built in the previous century.

Aerial view of 'Socach' Struan, showing the land at the Garry and Errochty confluence in the shape of a ploughshare.

St Fillan's Bell. (Courtesy of Perth Museum and Art Gallery).

St Fillan

In former times the church was known as the church of St Fillan and the footings of the old building can still be seen in the churchyard, to the south of the present building. It contained a statue of St Fillan, whose feet, in times of drought were dipped in the well of the same name at the foot of Tom an Tigh Mhor in order to bring much needed rain. The statue survived the Reformation until the minister, the Rev. John Hamilton, outraged by his parishioners' continuing belief in popish and pagan practices, took the statue and smashed it, flinging the broken pieces into the Garry! But it seems that he paid dearly for this deed, for soon afterwards his son died, quite insane. There is an ironic twist to this tale, as one of the cures attributed to St Fillan's Well, was that of insanity.

St Fillan's Market was held on the Saint's day, the first Friday in the new year (old style), about the 20th January , new style, in a field, immediately to the west of the church, called **Croft an Taggart** (priest's croft), and continued on, long after the Reformation.

The iron bell of St Fillan, measuring 10½ inches in height and 7 inches wide, was housed in the church and is a typical example of bells made in the very early times of the Celtic Church. It remained in use until the nineteenth century, when Mr McInroy of Lude presented the church with a new one. St Fillan's bell is now safely housed in Perth Museum.

There is a story attached to St Fillan's bell, as it was apparently stolen by a man from Rannoch who wished to transfer the reputed protection and privileges of the patron saint to his own district. Pausing in his flight home, at the top of Bohespic hill to rest a little, he placed the bell on a stone. When the time came to move on, the bell proved immovable - it was seemingly transfixed to the stone. Seeing this as a sign of the saint's displeasure, he immediately became alarmed and at once resolved to return the bell. As soon as he faced in the direction of Struan, the bell freed itself and was soon returned to its rightful place by its 'penitent bearer'.

In 1754 the loft of the old church was in need of repair as is shown in the Kirk Session minutes:

> Blair December 8th
> . . . Alex Stewart wright in Blairuachdar got a Portuguese piece of 36 shillings sterling of which he lent himself 7 sh 6d ster. more giving him 3sh 10d ster. for his workmanship & buying materials for the loft of Strowan. . .
>
> Blair Dec. 15th
> . . . Alex Stewart wright in Blairuachdar got nine shillings ster. of his workmanship for the loft of Strowan, so that the Session is yet due him £1.0.1½ ster. The smith got three shillings for workmanship. . .
>
> All this day's collection was given to the poor except half a crown to Duncan Stewart in Drumachine in part payment of the carriage of timber to the loft of Strowan and 14 shillings Scots to Charles Robertson in Auchinruie for a joist to the Bridge of Strowan. . .

In less than three years, trouble arose over the use of the loft and the damage caused:

> Strowan July 29th, 1757
> William McKenzie, miller at Strowan who with several others were making use of the loft of the church of Strowan and with that leaving the door open, was broken up by the wind which brought on charges upon the Session to the smith for mending the bands and nails and to said Donald McFarlane for timber in mending said door. . .
>
> Strowan Sept. 4th
> Wm McKenzie and John Forbes in Kirktown of Strowan paid a sixpence each and Tullich paid two pence and Patrick McLaren there is to pay a sixpence ster for making use of the loft of the church of Strowan indecently by putting their lint in it, so that as minuted, the doors and bands of said loft were broken. . .
>
> Blair Dec 20th 1761
> . . . and this day's collection amounting in both to £1.18.1 Scots which was given to William Young wright at Invervack for mending the two doors of the church of Strowan and furnishing timber and nails thereto. . .

St Fillan's appears to have been a dark, ill-lit church as the minutes of the Heritors' meeting on 8 December 1791 show:

> . . . whereas the pulpit in the church is badly lighted the meeting recommends to Mr McLagan [the minister] to cause a sky light of 4 panes of glass to be made where he thinks most proper. . .

A few months later there is a note that 15 shillings were spent 'for a sky light above the pulpit of Strowan. . .'

By the 1820s the old church was in a dilapidated state and so badly in need of repair that a new church was built, virtually on the same site, but a little to the side. It was designed in the first instance to hold 500 people, at a cost of £500, but was reduced in number to 450, including the gallery which ran round three sides, with an allowance of '18 inches for each sitter' and a vestry added.

Struan Church, built in 1828.

Preaching Stone in the churchyard at Struan.

The essence of the peacefulness of the church at Struan was summed up by the late Rev. Donald Cameron, for many years minister of the combined parish:

> . . . On that green knoll at the confluence of the Garry and the Errochty there is a sense of peace and the stillness that speaks to the hearing ear. It is a simple little church, quiet in its surroundings, suited to the environment and blending with one of the beautiful scenes in Scotland. . .

A little way to the front and right of the church door in the churchyard, is a 4 foot high pillar stone, with a simple cross incised on the east and west faces. It is thought to be a very old preaching stone, predating the existence of any formal church building.

Free Church

After the disruption in the Established Church of Scotland in the 1840s, the Free Church established their own place of worship opposite the Clachan Farm in 1855, to complement the Island Church south of Blair Atholl. A temporary wooden structure was built on land owned by a proprietor sympathetic to their beliefs and services were held on every third Sunday throughout the year. Up until this time, the Free Church congregation had had no place of shelter for their services, except for a barn to the rear of the Bruar Inn, where the proprietor allowed them to hold services in the winter.

In 1879 a stone church was built opposite the Clachan of Struan crossroads. A special pew was allocated to the Clachan of Struan family, whilst a block in the middle was reserved for the Calvine tenants. The church continued in use until the 1930s after which time it was used as a youth hostel. It has now been converted into a private house.

A cart track starts beside the church and climbs the 1,500 feet (460m) hill to Struan Point and **An Teampan** 787 653. Described as 'Temple of Struan' in old manuscripts, it is a mysterious place, a conspicuous knoll with commanding views of Glen Garry and the surrounding countryside. The top is ringed by an ancient dyke round which larch trees have been planted to form a circle. The

Sketch of the temporary wooden building which was used as the first Free Church in Struan.

trees on the windward side have disappeared, but those on the lee, though fallen, have taken root again and substantial growth has emanated from the toppled timber. The track continued on to a substantial peat moss used by the tenants in the area two hundred years ago. It was called the 'Custom Moss' as the tenants paid an annual 'custom' or fee to Colonel Robertson of Struan for its use.

Struan Bridge

The bridge across the Errochty at Old Struan. The former inn on the road to Tummelside is in the background.

Kindrochet (bridge head) relates to the bridge 709 653 across the Errochty Water below the church in Old Struan. The name would indicate that there has been a bridge here for a very long time. Minutes of the Kirk Session in the eighteenth century reveal the ongoing worries and concern over its state:

> Strowan March 8th 1719
> This day the Gentlemen of Sessions considering that the bridge on the Erochty was very dangerous for any person to cross, they did resolve to Petition his Grace the Duke of Atholl that his promise (for His Grace promised in Harvest 1718 to buy as much timber as would make a sufficient bridge; providing the tenents would lead [transport] it from Rannoch to the town of Strowan) to appoint his Factor at Blair Atholl to buy the timber and that they would lead it home and pay for the workmanship.
>
> September 21st 1746
> The Session considering that they have been at a great deal of Expences in repairing the Bridge of Strowan and that it is represented to them that the Bridge is like to be broken down by horses passing on it. . . Did therefore and hereby do appoint James McLaren in Kirktown of Strowan to exact two shg. Scots for every horse that passes on the said bridge after this date, and in case of refusal he is to seize and detain the horse until payment is made and report his diligence to the Session at every meeting in Strowan. . .
>
> Strowan December 2nd 1758
> . . . John Robertson in Tomberaggich gave a joist for the bridge of Struan valued at 14 sh. Scots which the Session takes to account in so much of his fine of fornication with Ann Robertson in Auchleeks. . .
>
> Strowan October 2nd 1763
> . . . Donald Moon at Bridge End of Tilt for his fornication with Margaret Robertson in Kincraigie was rebuked and given a communing for repairing the Bridge at Strowan.
>
> Strowan March 18th 1764
> . . . The Session appointed Patrick Stewart the officer in Toldunie to make a round thro' the braes of the parish in order to get men's subscriptions of their quota for building the bridge at Struan. . .

This serious effort to raise money to rebuild the bridge was supported by a petition on behalf of the tenants of Glen Errochty, Glen Garry, Invervack, Glen Fincastle and Strathtummel, dated 25 March 1765:

> A bridge on Water of Errochty at the Kirktown of Strowan would be of great advantage to the County of Atholl. This Water is rapid, sudden in rising, dangerous in crossing and frequently impassable whereby the communication betwixt the Braes and Strath is greatly interrupted.
>
> The inhabitants of the Glen of Fincastle and Strathtumble - a large tract of country, cross the water at above mentioned place going to and returning from their summer shealings.
>
> By want of a bridge access to Church and Churchyard and to a corn miln in the neighbourhood is rendered very difficult.

> Inhabitants of Glenerochty and Invervack a part of the annexed estate of Strowan share these disadvantages in common with the rest of the country but with an important difference that because of their nearness to Kirktown of Strowan, their occasions of crossing the water are more frequent and therefore the want of a bridge is more sensibly felt by them. . .
>
> An estimate had been made of building the Bridge wanted which is found to amount to £50 Ster. Heretors and farmers in the neighbourhood are so sensible of benefits that would redound to the Country by carrying this work into execution that they are willing to contribute one half of sum.

The £50 was duly raised, local lairds and people contributing half and the balance came through the factor of the annexed Struan Estate, Mr James Small. Thus the single arch stone bridge, the one that is still used today, was at last built:

> 18 February 1766
> Bond by Donald Forbes, mason in Duntanlich, as principal, and Donald Forbes and John Forbes in Foss, his cautioners, whereby, in consideration of the sum of £44 Stg. (of which one-half is to be paid by the commissioners for managing the Annexed Estates in Scotland by the hands of Captain James Small, factor on the Estate of Strowan, and one-half from the voluntary contributions of the neighbourhood), he binds himself to build and finish by 1st June next a sufficient arch with stone and lime over the Water of Erachty near the Kirktown of Strowan at or about where the present bridge now stands; which arch is to be 36 feet wide, 15 feet over walls breadth, 11 feet of a spring and 3 feet of height in the ledges of the arch. . .

Kindrochet Lodge 705 650 was the main dwelling of a cadet branch of the Robertsons of Struan and was rebuilt on the site of a much older house in 1816, the two wings being added after 1886, when the property was bought by the Atholl estate.

Clach an Druchsd (whooping cough stone) 816 652, stands in a natural birch wood, beside a sheep fank, about two hundred yards east of Easter Kindrochet. The stone measures about 4

The Whooping Cough Stone with natural cleft which holds about half a gallon of water.

feet 6 inches in length and about 2 feet high, with a natural cleft in the top which holds about half a gallon of water. As late as 1860, mothers were still bringing their children, sick with whooping cough, to this stone, to drink the water, but only from a spoon made from the horn of a living cow. There was no cure without that!

Auchanruidh (field of the shieling) 795 639 is about a mile west of Kindrochet Lodge, along the old road on the south side of the river. Duncan McDonald was the tenant here in 1853 and agreed with the estate to build a new dwelling house, which cost £45 for mason work. Threshing equipment was installed in a barn where, until recently, the remains of a horse-gang platform could be seen on the outside. Here, two horses walking round provided the power to drive the machinery in the shed through underground gearing and this system continued on until well into this century.

The horsegang platform for powering the threshing mill at Auchanruidh, which was in use up to the 1920s.

The old ford linking Auchanruidh and Cuiltaloskin, with the former footbridge in the background.

Bore Stone

A square-shaped, dressed granite stone lies on its side below the front of the house, in the north west corner of the old garden. In one of its sides is a 3 ½ inch diameter hole about 6 inches deep, probably for holding a flag staff. It is recorded that at one time the stone stood on a nearby knoll to the east of the house, but was removed when the knoll was levelled in the 1860s. This particular knoll would have had a commanding view of the glen to the west and eastwards to Glen Garry and it is very likely that this 'bore stone' held a flag or standard as a signal to the local inhabitants, perhaps even as a rallying point for the Clan Donnachaidh.

Before the bridge was built to link Auchanruidh with today's glen road, there was a ford a short distance upstream, leading to **Cuiltaloskin** (nook of toads) 792 642. Angus Robertson was living here in 1760 and the problems he was causing the neighbourhood were outlined in a memorandum by James Small:

> Angus Robertson, ordered to be removed form Cuiltaloskin went to Blair Atholl and complained to Lord Prestongrange and you cannot imagine what disorder he has occasioned by telling a number of lyes to his neighbours of what great things my Lord promised him. All I can say is that by order he had a year and a half ago a warning to provide for himself. He is a bankrupt and was owing three years' rent till he was warned. Besides his wife is a very bad neighbour.

Later that year, Angus Robertson left the village. In 1820 a tenant by name of Ann Gow caused so

The bore stone at Auchanruidh which might have carried a signal flag.

much trouble with her neighbours that the laird was forced to write and warn her:

> I hereby agree that you will not be removed from the house that you built at Cultaloskin as long as you conduct yourself as a quiet and peaceable neighbour.

Ann wrote a song in 1827 about going to the Lowlands to work in the harvest and from it it appears that she much preferred weaving tartans, for which she was noted, than working in the south.

The substantial remains of **Tulloch** (hill) 775 635 are still clearly seen about a mile further up the glen on the south side. John Fleming, a tenant in 1680, insisted that his sasine of the land clearly showed him to be a vassal of the Marquis of Atholl. However, Robertson of Struan vigorously disagreed and 'broke out on Fleming with passionate violence, calling him a rascal, knave and villain'. Then, thrusting his hand into his jacket, where he kept his dirk and pistol, he said, 'he did not know what held his hand from writing his name on Fleming's face'. Struan went on to say he would see the Marquis hanged before he would be vassal and the Privy Council, finding the charge proven, sentenced him to a term of imprisonment until he craved pardon on his knees.

Eleven Sons of Blairfettie

Blairfettie (whistling plain) 750 643 is a further mile along the glen and is now a large farm and summer garden centre. At one time it was occupied by a Robertson laird who had eleven sons, ten of whom were stalwart Highlanders, but the eleventh was a fair-haired, sickly child. One day the brothers set off on a deer hunting expedition on Tulloch Hill (opposite) and paused at **Cragan Liath Mor** (big grey crag) 757 619. Some of the deerhounds started fighting, the brothers wagering on the outcome and a fierce quarrel developed between two of them. Like the dogs, they agreed to fight it out, with five ranged on each side and the upshot was, that in the end, all ten lay dead. The youngest brother, who had taken no part in the contest, returned home to break the news to his father, who died of grief soon after. A rough stone was erected on Cragan Liath to mark the site of the fatal struggle.

In the early part of the eighteenth century, Patrick Robertson succeeded to the Blairfettie estate, at about the time the Duke of Atholl's Fencibles were formed. In 1705 Blairfettie provided thirteen men: seven tenants, a tailor and five servants. Patrick's standing with the Duke flourished at this time and in 1711 he was appointed to be forester between Glen Edendon and the head of Loch Garry. His instructions were as follows:

> He is to kill 8 deer at least for His G's use, and to preserve the birch Woods on both sides of the Water of Garrie from being destroyed & cut away by tenants of the property, except for the use of their biggings allenarly [only], and bring prisoner to Blair Castle any he shall find peeling standing trees, & for his encouragement and pains in preserving the deer and said woods he is allowed to kill yearly for his own use, any lame deer he shall find within the said bounds.

Patrick gained further recognition for his loyal services, when, in the same year, he was charged with maintaining law and order. Both he and Donald Robertson of Auchleeks were empowered to:

> . . . exact 12d Scots for each cow or ox coming from the north to the south for sale which shall stay a night on any part of our property north of Water of Tummel.

Patrick's only son, James, 'Blairfettie Younger', was named in an order signed by the 1st Duke on 3 October 1711, to appear in court in Dunkeld:

> . . . to cite Blairpheatie younger, and James Robertson, late butler and others to compear att ane court to be holden at Dunkeld Fryday come eight days to answer for presuming to go into the Castle of Blair Atholl on 23rd last, after His Grace's removal from thence that day, with strangers and destroying some of the furniture of the same. . .

The outcome of this incident is not known but in later years James's sympathies lay with the Jacobite cause and in 1745 he joined the army commanded by Lord George Murray, brother of the 2nd Duke and was appointed Major in command of the second battalion of the Atholl Brigade.

As the Jacobite army retreated towards Inverness early in 1746, government troops under the Duke of Cumberland followed, and he stationed sixty men from the Argyllshire Highlanders at Blairfettie. These troops insulted and maltreated Lady Blairfettie by forcing her to wait upon them at table and keeping her children, who were ill with whooping cough 'upon short commons'. In desperation she despatched a herd boy in secret to find her husband in Inverness and give him the message of their plight. On receipt of the news, he gathered a force of Robertson men and arrived at Blairfettie at midnight, taking the sentry by surprise and entering the house before the Argyllshire men realised what was happening but they put up a strong resistance before finally surrendering.

When Lady Blairfettie came downstairs she saw the garrison disarmed and held prisoner in the dining room, with a dozen of her husband's followers standing guard over them with drawn swords. Her husband was incensed at the way his wife and family had been treated and was determined to mete out the harshest punishment but his wife begged for leniency. Nevertheless, Blairfettie House was razed to the ground shortly afterwards by government troops.

The 1638 roll of the heritors in the 'Parochin of Strowane' tells us that:

> . . . Auld Chairlis Robertson of Achleikis had twelve men with gunes, bowis, sheaves, swirdis and Tairges.

In 1746 the Auchleeks laird, Duncan Robertson served in the Atholl Brigade as Captain and was wounded at Culloden. The Atholl Brigade held the right flank of the Jacobite army and inflicted the greatest damage on government troops.

March with Atholl

The boundaries of the Auchleeks and Blairfettie estates tended to follow natural features like watersheds, ridges and streams and were generally trouble-free except when problems of grazing or ownership of peat mosses arose. The northern boundary of these two estates marched with the Atholl ground of Achlany and for about a mile it needed careful marking. The top of the ridge is flat and featureless, was used by all parties

Boundary stone engraved with 'A' on the Atholl/Robertson march.

for grazing and there was also a peat moss nearby. In the 1860s Auchleeks maintained that the area known as Cor-na-Galig, below the watershed on the Atholl side was a commonty but the arbiter called in to settle the dispute maintained he could not substantiate this claim and that the march was the line as agreed in the previous century. This was outlined by boundary stones, marked on the north side with 'A' and with 'R' to the south, and the first of these is on the Black Knowe. It was here that Alex McDonald of Achlany dug his peat. From here the line ran due west for 743 yards, along the top of the 'Knobs' to the next stone at the Bothy Knowe, named after a hut known as the 'Smugglers' Bothy', in which illicit whisky was distilled. John Macfarlane, a witness called to testify in the boundary dispute, remembered making whisky there 30 years earlier. All this while the boundary marched with Blairfettie, but at the corner it reached Auchleeks land. At the Bothy Knowe the boundary swept due north for a distance of 303 yards to another stone suitably

Boundary stone engraved with 'R' on the Atholl/Robertson march.

incised 'A' and 'R'. From here the boundary continued in a straight line to the summit of Fiackhil More, a distance of 579 yards and another finely-shaped and marked stone next to the metal post and wire fence erected in the 1860s. The final stone is only 157 yards distant at the corner of the Achlany march where it headed north to the Garry and here there is a beautifully inscribed stone with 'A' and 'R' carved into it.

The Glen School

The **Glen Errochty School** 733 646 was located between Tomcraggach and Dalchalloch and the field across the road is still known as the 'Schoolhouse field'. It was one of six schools set up by William Ramsay, the first annexed estates factor in a effort to 'civilise' the inhabitants, who, according to him, were noted for their 'barbarity, thieving and rebellion'. In 1755 the school had 34 pupils learning reading and writing, while the girls were taught knitting, sewing and spinning. All the boys worked in the fields in summer and the girls in domestic service, so the school opened only in the winter months, from November to May. Patrick MacLaren was paid £4 for six months' teaching and in a petition drawn up by the parents, it was stated that as he prayed with his pupils at church, this had a beneficial affect on their morals. The parents also insisted that their children 'lose in summer a great part of what they learn in winter' and so the factor agreed to year-round teaching and he was paid an extra £3.

In 1771 the Glen Errochty schoolmaster, Archibald McDiarmid, submitted a petition to the factor:

> November last your Lordships' factor having been informed that the petitioner was deficient in his duties as schoolmaster particularly in not attending to teach children in summer and harvest was pleased to dismiss me from office. Petitioner admits the last part of the charge against him is true and proceeded from two reasons: During the summer and harvest months few scholars did or could attend and the petitioner was ignorant of the order by the Board of 14th March 1759 by which attendance of the schoolmaster then for the whole year is commended and there is £3 of additional salary allowed the petitioner's predecessor upon this condition. As he hoped there is no immorality or any glaring faults to be laid to his charge and as he engages to give his attendance the whole year he humbly hopes the Hon. Board will be pleased to restore him to his office especially as tenants have now signified to the factor they are satisfied and that the Petitioner has no other way of making his bread, especially as he had not time given him to provide for himself till so near the term.

The factor relented, and deciding that Archibald McDiarmid 'seems to be sensible of his fault', he had 'no objection to his being deponed to his office.'

Trinafour Inn

Trinafour (third of the pasture) 725 646 was another Robertson property, at the junction of the glen road and the military road from Dalnacardoch to Tummel Bridge, which was completed in 1730. Soon after this, the Trinafour Inn opened for the benefit of passing travellers and in 1757, Patrick Robertson was granted a licence for the retailing of 'ale, beer and other excisable liquors'. John Stewart was appointed landlord in 1825, after being evicted from Strathgroy Farm and Frederick Graham, the factor, wrote that he had:

> . . . fortunately succeeded in getting rid of John Stewart in time to prevent the ruin of the farm and to put a stop in that neighbourhood to any further effects of his swindling propensities. He has shown himself utterly incorrigible which Mr Robertson [Auchleeks] will find out before Stewart has long been tenant of Trinafour Inn which he has taken.

Trinafour House, the former inn, showing the extension built in the 1890s.

A notable Perthshire dame, the Dowager Lady Menzies, was a frequent traveller towards the end of last century between her residence at Rannoch Lodge and Struan railway station, twenty five miles away. On one occasion, when returning from Struan, her carriage overturned at a precipitous part of the road above Mullinavaddie, so that she, the post boy and the contents of the carriage rolled down the hillside into a bog. All escaped injury but the driver found it difficult to explain the profusion of bottles, half bottles and noggins that were scattered all over the place. Lady Menzies was in complete ignorance that the driver was employed in 'running the cutter', that is in transporting 'much needed' supplies to her drouthy employees! On her next journey she insisted on a change of driver and was assured that Duncan, the replacement, was an exceptionally sober, steady man who never went near a roadside inn. The journey progressed uneventfully as far as the Trinafour Inn, located at a loop on the road, where, when the carriage arrived, the horses, much to Duncan's dismay, pulled strongly to the left, as if to make their accustomed stop! To have his newly acquired reputation destroyed by a pair of stubborn horses was too much for Duncan, so he tugged and whipped with all his might, until he succeeded in keeping them to the main road, uttering between each cut of his lash 'You tam' [damn'd] liars!'

By the 1820s the inn was renamed Auchleeks and closed in the 1890s when it became the main residence of the Robertsons of Auchleeks. They renamed it Trinafour House and built on a large extension, which was taken down in the 1960s.

Trinafour Post Office

A post office was opened in Trinafour in 1846 and a regular postal service was established the following year:

> I submit an official Post may be established from Calvine (under Blair Atholl) to serve Glenerrochty, Auchleeks and Trinafour, the number of letters for this district exceeding 100 in a week, the expense of the measure to be 9/– a week for a footman and £4 a year for a Receiver at Trinafour.

Trinafour post office ceased operating in the 1980s.

Trinafour Post office, formerly Auchleeks Post office, in the 1920s. The wooden building was taken down a few years ago when the post office closed.

William Robertson, driver of the Rannoch mail coach, setting off from Struan in the last century.

A Trinafour tenant, John MacGregor, petitioned the Commission for the Annexed Estates in 1763 for the post of Inspector and Surveyor of yarn for the district:

> That the petitioner had been in the practice of raising flax in the Ground for many years which succeeded with him beyond expectation, also in carrying on spinning and selling Linnen Yarn to traveling Merchants in the Country.
>
> That the petr. is informed that your Honours have been pleased to give so many hogsheads of Lint seed to the possessors of Strowans Estate and Loch Garrys Estate in order to encourage that branch of Cultivation and Manufactory.
>
> That the petr. is likewise credibly informed that your Honours proposes to appoint and sett an inspector or surveyor to examine the yarn that it may be regularly & fairly Reeled and counted, and properly sorted as to the Colour and Quality of the Lint and yarn to prevent fraud and deceit agreeable to the Act of Parliament made for that purpose.
>
> That the petr. most humbly hopes, that your Honours will be pleased to sett and appoint in the Charge of Surveying and Inspecting all Linnen Yarn in these Countrys, and for keeping proper Regulation amongst the tennants and the traveling Merchants who purchase their yarn. . .

Mullinavaddie Mill

Mullinavaddie (mill of the wolf) 713 610 is named after the place where the last wolf in Perthshire was reputedly killed. The tradition is that Mrs Robertson, the miller's wife, was baking in her kitchen, when a ravenous wolf entered through the open door and seeing a six-month old baby in its cradle in the corner, began to drag it outside. When Mrs Robertson saw what was happening, she grabbed hold of a stout wooden potato masher and struck the wolf on the head several times, killing it outright.

There are still substantial remains of the mill beside the stream, with evidence of broken millstones scattered around. John Cummin was the miller in 1753 and he and the mill tenants were engaged in bringing a millstone down the hill, when it toppled and fell across a stream which formed the boundary with the Atholl land of Bohespic. When they returned a few days later to move it, Cummin, to his dismay, found the Bohespic tenant, Donald Stewart, waiting for him, who indicated that as the stone lay across the boundary, half of it was rightfully his and demanded it be cut in half. To safeguard the millstone, the miller had to agree grudgingly to free Donald Stewart from paying any mill dues for the following three years!

Shieling Disturbance

An area of land a few miles to the north of Trinafour was the subject of a boundary dispute in the last century because it contained a valuable peat moss as well as pasture good enough to graze five hundred sheep. The Atholl Estate claimed the land outright, while the Robertsons of Auchleeks asserted that it was common grazing. In 1800 a lease was granted to William Stewart, giving him the right to graze his cattle and horses on the shieling of **Fevora** (shieling of the lord's bog) 727 682 and the footings of a shieling bothy there are still in evidence. In a report on a march dispute in 1781, Duncan Robertson testified that about fifty years earlier, a bothy had been built on the pasture and rebuilt twenty years later when the tenant only stayed a year, 'as the people of Glengarry threatened him for coming so near them.' In 1773 two Auchleeks tenants, Duncan MacGregor and Alexander Macintosh built shiel houses there, which the Atholl ground officer wanted to throw down as he alleged they were on Atholl land. He reported that:

> Since that time, Auchleeks comes in person and builds a sheal house on Feavoragh and pastures his cattle much further down on the grasings of Glengarry so that there is no saying when he will give up encroaching if not prevented.

In 1826 Auchleeks rebuilt the bothy and wrote:

> The bothy at Fevoragh is nothing more than rebuilding of an old one which has always stood on the same spot. This bothy was put up

Substantial ruins of the Mullinavaddie corn mill. The mill dam and lade can be easily found nearby.

> on my orders last year to accomodate my people and belonged to my grandfather and great grandfather and has stood there from time immemorial.

The following year Dalnacardoch sheep were constantly being moved off the pasture by Auchleeks tenants, who in the month of August, removed 2,000 loads of peats from the moss, leading the Atholl factor to observe that Auchleeks wanted to conserve his own peat stocks at Atholl's expense. Lieutenant Duncan Robertson of Dalnamein had his peats broken up in 1828 while Peter Robertson from Dalinturuaine, who had been cutting peat for twenty years, had them thrown back into the moss. The boundary dispute was settled in 1829 in favour of Auchleeks.

Robert Robertson, 9th laird of Auchleeks, was born in 1777 and died in 1859.

An early Clan Donnachaidh chief can claim no glory for being the subject of the final story in the book. He married a wealthy young girl who produced a lovely daughter and made a comfortable home, but slowly feelings between them cooled, perhaps because she did not provide him with a son. He coldly decided he must be rid of her and knowing that **Loch Chon** (loch of the dog) 690 679 was one of her favourite places, selected it as the place to carry out his evil deed. Saying he had a surprise for her, he invited her one day to accompany him to Loch Chon and being unaware of any evil intent, she agreed to go with him. Once on the island he led her into an underground cavern, where he tied her to a stake and blocked the entrance so that her cries for help would go unheard. The chief felt no remorse and was soon off to woo the daughter of the Thane of Glen Tilt, who, on asking if the chief was already married, received the answer that he could swear in all honesty that no wife of his was above ground.

Aerial view of Loch Chon from the west, showing the island where a chief of Clan Donnachaidh carried out an ingeniously evil plan to be rid of his wife.

SOURCES AND BIBLIOGRAPHY

1. MANUSCRIPT SOURCES

Charter Room, Blair Castle – John Crerar manuscript; factors' notes and memos; letters; rentals; maps and plans.
Fergusson, J. L. F, Moulin – Calendar of Baledmund Charters, 1328 – 1811.
National Library of Scotland, Edinburgh – Delvine Papers, Baron Court of Faskally records 1662 – 1743.
General Register Office for Scotland – Baron Court of Lude records; Church of Scotland records, Minutes of Heritors' meetings; Minutes of Kirk Session of Blair Atholl & Struan parish; Minutes of SSPCK; Forfeited Estates papers, Struan and Lochgarry.
Robertson, James Irvine, Aberfeldy – Questions put to Donald Stewart in 1818 by Mr Irvine, minister of Little Dunkeld.
Post Office Records, London – Trinafour / Auchleeks post office.

2. PUBLICATIONS

ATHOLL, JOHN 7TH DUKE of – *Chronicles of the Atholl & Tullibardine Families 1908.*
BOWSTEAD, CHRISTOPHER – *Facts and Fancies about Kilmaveonaig* 1915.
COOK, HENRY – *Clan Donnachaidh Annual*: Bruar's Place in Military History 1972.
CUNNINGHAM, ALEC – *Tales of Rannoch* 1989.
DIXON, JOHN – *Pitlochry Past and Present* 1925.
DWELLY, EDWARD – *Illustrated Gaelic – English Dictionary* 1967.
FERGUSSON, CHARLES – *Transactions of the Gaelic Society of Inverness*: Sketches of the early History, Legends and Traditions of Strathardle and its Glens, Volumes XV, XVIII, XIX and XX.
FERGUSSON, JAMES – *Records of the Clan and Names of Fergusson, Ferguson and Fergus 1895.*
HART-DAVIS, DUFF – *Monarchs of the Glen* 1978.
KERR, JOHN – *Transactions of the Gaelic Society of Inverness*: Old Grampian Highways Vol. XLIX; Old Roads to Strathardle Vol. LI; Wade in Atholl Vol. LIII; East by Tilt Vol. LIV; Water Mills of Atholl Vol. LV; Robertsons of Glen Errochty Vol. LVI; Nomina-A Journal of Name Studies Relating to Great Britain and Ireland; Atholl Shieling Names 1987; Along an Atholl Boundary 1989/90; The Stewarts (The Stewart Society); The Stewarts of Strathgarry 1988; The Stewarts of Shierglas 1989; Clan Donnachaidh Annual; The Clan Lands of Invervack 1991; Highland Highways 1991; Queen Victoria's Scottish Diaries 1992.
MARSHALL, WILLIAM – *Historic Scenes in Perthshire* 1880.
MELDRUM, REV. A – *Clan Donnachaidh Annual:* Lady Lude of the '45. 1977/78.
MUNRO, DR JEAN – *Clan Donnachaidh Annual:*Two Famous Robertson Harps 1968.
O'MURCHU, MAIRTIN – *East Perthshire Gaelic* 1989.
PENNANT, THOMAS – *A Tour in Scotland* 1769 1979.
Proceedings of the Society of Antiquaries – Primitive Scottish Bells Vol. 1; Pictish Brooch from Aldclune Vol. 115.
ROBERTSON, JAMES IRVINE – *Random Shots* 1990
SALMOND, J.B. – *The Old Stalker and Other Verses* 1936.
Scots Magazine – *Cam Ye by Atholl.*
SCROPE, WILLIAM – *The Art of Deer Stalking* 1839.

INDEX